Embodied Testimonies, Gendered Memories, and the Poetics of Trauma

Exploring the Intersection of Deconstructionist and Postcolonial Trauma Theory

Edited by

Maryam Ghodrati

University of Massachusetts Amherst

Rachel Dale

Brandeis University

Series in Sociology

 VERNON PRESS

www.vernonpress.com

In the Americas:	*In the rest of the world:*
Vernon Press	Vernon Press
1000 N West Street, Suite 1200	C/Sancti Espiritu 17,
Wilmington, Delaware, 19801	Malaga, 29006
United States	Spain

Series in Sociology

Library of Congress Control Number: 2023950781

ISBN: 979-8-8819-0173-8

Also available: 978-1-64889-824-2 [Hardback]; 979-8-8819-0019-9 [PDF, E-Book]

Content Warning:
Due to the sensitive nature of the topics addressed in this collection,
there are references and images that some readers might find
disturbing. Please use your discretion as you proceed.

Table of Contents

List of Figures

Introduction

Maryam Ghodrati

University of Massachusetts Amherst

Rachel Dale

Brandeis University

As a new clinical student, Arthur Kleinman vividly recalls an emotionally charged incident in his book *The Illness Narratives: Suffering, Healing, and the Human Condition*. The patient was a misfortunate seven-year-old girl who had suffered extensive burns over most of her body. Her treatment involved the daily torment of a whirlpool bath, during which the medical team meticulously tweezed away the burnt flesh from her raw wounds. This excruciating routine was marked by the girl's screams, moans, and desperate pleas for the medical team to halt the painful procedure. Kleinman's responsibility was to hold her uninjured hand, offering her solace, while also assisting the surgical resident in swiftly removing the dead and infected tissue from her fragile body in the water, which gradually transformed from a pinkish to bloody red hue.

In an attempt to distract the young patient from her traumatic encounters with intense pain, Kleinman engaged her in conversations about her home, family, and school. He found it difficult to bear witness to the daily horrors, including the girl's piercing screams, the sight of dead tissue floating in the blood-stained water, the peeling flesh, the oozing wounds, and the ongoing struggles involved in the cleaning and bandaging process. However, one day, out of desperation and a sense of helplessness, Kleinman implored the girl to share her experiences and how she managed to endure the agonizing burns and the repetitive surgical ritual. To Kleinman's astonishment, the girl paused, her disfigured face making it challenging to discern her expression, but then proceeded to explain straightforwardly and directly. As she narrated her experiences, she held onto Kleinman's hand firmly, no longer screaming or resisting the surgeon or the nurse. As their bond grew strong and trust was established, the girl took it upon herself to share her experiences every day, enabling the student to develop a deeper comprehension. By the time the student's training in the rehabilitation unit concluded, a noticeable improvement was observed in the girl's ability to tolerate the debridement process.[1]

The opening anecdote in Kleinman's narrative and its subsequent exploration in this collection serve as a compelling theoretical testing ground. The memory of the excruciating event, which involved the young girl being badly burned, and its harrowing aftermath, regardless of the underlying context in which this event occurred, becomes the young girl's sole means of establishing a fragile connection with the outside world. Paradoxically, the well-intentioned efforts of the medical team to divert and distract inadvertently exacerbate her isolation and intensify her suffering. The example of the young girl underscores fundamental concepts and areas of contention within trauma theory, particularly the notion that trauma eludes effective expression through language and the deep sense of isolation and alienation it induces.

The girl's traumatic experience resonates with two fundamental hypotheses that have shaped the theoretical foundation for this collection and have perhaps given rise to deconstructivist trauma theory that, consequently, has been critically examined by postcolonial trauma theorists. One hypothesis, proposed by Elaine Scarry, posits that physical pain eludes linguistic capture, relegating those in pain to an "invisible geography" where their cries reverberate like "intergalactic screams" for those who bear witness. The second hypothesis this anecdote brings into focus is Cathy Caruth's notion of unassimilated experiences of trauma. Here, the girl's memory and ongoing suffering exemplify the enduring impact of the traumatic event on her body and psyche, corresponding to both Scarry's notion of physical and Caruth's assertion of psychological pain's resistance to language.

This collection of articles is committed to exploring the confluence of pluralist/postcolonial critique and deconstructivist psychoanalysis, which represent the two primary theoretical frameworks for understanding traumatic experiences and their representation. Through this exploration, the collection aims to illuminate the limitations observed in non-Western portrayals of traumatic history while also addressing the complicity of Western colonial and imperial powers in perpetuating human suffering. By emphasizing the unspeakable experiences of individuals as the foundation for collective and socio-political engagement, the book challenges established postcolonial trauma theory. Such theory often places excessive emphasis on the collective nature of traumatic experiences, submerging individual narratives beneath ideological constructs of nationalism and self-determination. However, it is important to acknowledge the imperative of decolonizing trauma studies by

---

[1] Arthur Kleinman, The Illness Narratives: Suffering, Healing, and the Human Condition (New York: Basic Books, 1989), xi-xii.

examining the social and political factors that contribute to these individual experiences of trauma, particularly in relation to gender, in favor of dominant narratives and power structures.

Elaine Scarry, who has written extensively on topics such as beauty, pain, war, and the body, explores – in her 1985 influential work *The Body in Pain: The Making and Unmaking of the World* – the nature of physical pain and its social, cultural, and political implications. She has suggested that if one were to consider the range of emotional, perceptual, and somatic experiences associated with various objects or states, the list would be extensive. However, this list would come to an abrupt halt when encountering physical pain. Unlike other conscious experiences, physical pain lacks referential content and does not pertain to or signify anything external. It is precisely because physical pain cannot be objectified outside of the human body that it resists linguistic expression more strongly than any other phenomenon. Its elusive nature and inability to be fully conveyed through words make it uniquely challenging to articulate. Pain, as Scarry asserts, not only resists language but "actively destroys it."[2] Its resistance to objectification leaves persons in pain, deprived of the resources of speech. Pain that occurs in other people's bodies "flicker before the mind, then disappear," making this "absolute split between one's sense of one's reality and the reality of another person."[3]

The story of the young girl under the care of a medical team, however, extends beyond the realm of physical trauma to encompass the memory of an event, highlighting the complex nature of her experience. Furthermore, this is why Scarry's profound insights into the limitations of language when confronted with physical pain find a compelling resonance in the work of the prominent literary trauma theorist Cathy Caruth. In her seminal work *Unclaimed Experience: Trauma, Narrative, and History*, Caruth delves into a similar challenge of comprehending and representing traumatic experiences, albeit with a focus on psychological trauma. She emphasizes the inherent difficulty in truly listening, knowing and capturing the essence of such crises. Drawing parallels to Scarry's argument on the resistance of pain to linguistic expression, Caruth acknowledges the elusive nature of trauma, which disrupts conventional narrative structures and eludes easy comprehension. She posits that the language employed to address psychological crises often assumes a literary quality, one that defies our understanding even as it seeks to convey the depths of trauma. Caruth's exploration of trauma and its impact on storytelling enriches our understanding of the girl's incommunicable pain and the difficulties encountered by Kleinman

---

[2] Elaine Scarry, The Body in Pain: The Making and Unmaking of the World (New York: Oxford University Press, 1985), 4.
[3] Ibid., 3.

and the medical team in truly apprehending her experience. It illuminates a fundamental challenge that emerges when striving to engage with and comprehend traumatic encounters.

Caruth's proposition that this language "defies, even as it claims, our understanding"[4] finds support in the psychoanalytic hypothesis put forth by the prominent psychiatrist of the late nineteenth century, Pierre Janet. According to Janet, there is a distinction between normal memory, which involves the act of constructing a coherent narrative, and traumatic memory, which manifests as a frozen fixation on an event that has not yet been comprehended and sorted as a linear and meaningful story. Normal memory, much like other psychological phenomena, is an active process specifically characterized by the act of narrating a story, as Janet explains. Its resolution is not complete until we achieve not only an outward response through our actions but also an internal response through the words, we speak to ourselves and the organization of the narrative we recount to others. It is through the integration of this recital into our personal history that a situation can be satisfactorily resolved. Therefore, strictly speaking, an individual who clings to a fixed idea of an event cannot be considered to possess a "memory" in the true sense. The term "traumatic memory" is used merely for "convenience."[5]

Drawing upon the psychoanalytic differentiation of normal memory and traumatic memory, Geoffrey Hartman's theoretical insights provide a deeper understanding of the intricate interplay between language and trauma within the realm of literary theory. According to Hartman, trauma theory focuses on the "relationship of words and trauma," helping us to "read the wound" with the aid of literature. In an insightful observation, he states that there is "always a disjunction between experience and understanding of it" and that "literary theory/knowledge finds the 'real,' identifies with it, and attempts to bring it back [into focus]. The language of this literary construction of trauma is not literal; it is a different sort of statement that relates to that negative moment in experience that cannot be or has not been adequately experienced."[6] This definition sheds light on that moment of the extreme, the shock of a loss, witnessing a brutal blow, and extreme pain that defeats tolerance, comprehension, and, therefore, language. There is a reality that trauma and literary theory have helped to identify: a moment of experience "experienced

---

[4] Cathy Caruth, Unclaimed Experience: Trauma, Narrative, and History (Baltimore: Johns Hopkins University Press, 1996), 5.

[5] Pierre Janet quoted in Judith Herman, Trauma and Recovery: The Aftermath of Violence – From Domestic Abuse to Political Terror (New York: Basic Books, 1997), 35.

[6] Geoffrey H. Hartman, "On Traumatic Knowledge and Literary Studies," New Literary History 26, no. 3 (1995): 540.

too soon and too unexpectedly,"[7] as Cathy Caruth states before the subject is there to receive it consciously.

The concept of incommunicability and unspeakability surrounding traumatic experiences, as well as the challenges in comprehending the events and their aftermath for both the listener and the witness, has been closely linked to the deconstructivist Yale school of thought. Emerging in the 1990s, trauma theory drew upon Freudian concepts of repression, dissociation, disruption, and repetition compulsion. Pioneered by scholars such as Cathy Caruth, Shoshana Felman, and Geoffrey Hartman, these post-structuralist thinkers employed deconstructionist theory to examine trauma and its representation. Central to their investigations was the identification of dissociative symptoms experienced universally by trauma survivors. Caruth posited that trauma constituted an insoluble problem of the unconscious, exposing inherent contradictions within both experience and language.[8] This dissociation of consciousness arises from the terror and surprise encountered during specific events, rendering meaningful recollection and the normal integration of the original experience unattainable for the subject. The delayed nature of reflection, recurrence of symptoms, and reliving of the experience, among other manifestations, stem directly from the absence of consciousness at the moment of the traumatic event. This neurobiological and psychological response elucidates the sufferer's inability to comprehend and articulate their experience, leading to belated recollections that indirectly and somewhat distortedly recall the past.

Caruth and Hartman offer a framework for understanding history through an examination of delayed responses and "other intrusive phenomena."[9] They argue that exploring the manifestations of trauma in victims enables us to grasp the implications of trauma for the individual and contextualize it within the surrounding historical backdrop. Caruth perceives the testimonies of victims and survivors as markers of trauma's effects, serving as acts of "departure," signifying the act of walking away, surviving, and managing the repercussions of the experience. At the core of a trauma narrative, Caruth argues, there resides a form of dual storytelling characterized by the oscillation between a crisis of death and the corresponding crisis of life. It involves recounting the unbearable nature of the event itself alongside the equally unbearable nature of its survival.[10] This inherent doubleness contributes to the literary nature of

---

[7] Caruth, Unclaimed Experience, 101.

[8] Michelle Balaev, Contemporary Approaches in Literary Trauma Theory (New York: Palgrave, 2014), 1.

[9] Caruth, Unclaimed Experience, 11.

[10] Ibid., 7.

trauma discourse, reflecting the challenge of expressing not merely what occurred but rather how it was felt.

Contrasting the prevailing poststructuralist perspectives on trauma, Michael Balaev offers a more nuanced and pragmatic stance by challenging the asocial and apolitical nature of deconstructivist theories. While scholars like Caruth perceive trauma as an unsolvable issue rooted in the unconscious, Balaev raises concerns regarding the depiction of the past as a void for trauma sufferers and the ambiguity of language referencing absence.[11] Balaev's viewpoint aligns with that of postcolonial critics, including Laurie Vickroy, Kali Tal, Stef Craps, Irene Visser, and clinical practitioner Judith Herman, who emphasize the social, cultural, and political particularities of traumatic experiences. They argue against the Caruthian perspective, which they believe portrays trauma victims as devoid of autonomy and agency, thereby negating the potential for understanding history through trauma narratives.

In their critique of poststructuralist approaches to trauma narratives, Balaev asserts that the meaning of trauma can be located rather than permanently lost, as it is intertwined with larger social, political, and economic practices that influence violence.[12] Similarly, Herman and Vickroy propose that trauma is socially induced, and they highlight the empirical foundations of trauma, including the ongoing connections to "global political movements for human rights" that facilitate the ability to articulate the inexpressible.[13] By challenging the decontextualized view of trauma, these scholars shed light on the social dimensions of traumatic experiences, emphasizing the significance of historical and political contexts. Their perspectives offer an alternative lens through which to examine trauma narratives, acknowledging the interconnectedness between personal experiences and broader socio-political forces.

In her groundbreaking 2015 article titled "Decolonizing Trauma Theory: Retrospect and Prospects," Irene Visser examines the emergence of a new wave in trauma studies. She argues for the development of a decolonized trauma theory in response to the influential special issue of Studies in the Novel published in Spring/Summer 2008. This special issue, edited by Gert Buelens and Stef Craps, focuses on decolonizing trauma theory and emphasizes the importance of including non-Western and non-European experiences, such as racism and the ongoing everyday suffering of marginalized groups.[14] Visser's

---

[11] Balaev, Contemporary Approaches, 1.

[12] Ibid., 8.

[13] Herman, Trauma and Recovery; Laurie Vickroy, Trauma and Survival in Contemporary Fiction (Charlottesville: University of Virginia Press, 2002).

[14] Irene Visser, "Decolonizing Trauma Theory: Retrospect and Prospects," Humanities 4, no. 2 (2015): 250.

abstract highlights the need for an inclusive approach to trauma that incorporates non-Western belief systems, rituals, and ceremonies. She asserts that embracing these cultural perspectives is essential to achieving the remaining objectives of the long-standing project of decolonizing trauma theory.[15] Quoting Craps, Visser points out that trauma studies must take into account social and historical relations and situate the traumatic histories of subordinate groups within the broader context of socially dominant groups.[16]

Drawing from Luckhurst's critique, Visser examines Caruth's Freudian perspective on trauma, which tends to focus on the lasting effects of trauma and the maintenance of the post-traumatic condition.[17] Visser suggests that Dominick LaCapra's work provides steps toward overcoming the ahistorical grip of Freudian/Caruthian trauma theory. LaCapra challenges the notion that melancholia and fragility are defining and unchangeable characteristics of the post-traumatic stage. Instead, he emphasizes the importance of strengthening communal and individual identities to counteract the lasting effects of trauma.[18] Visser concludes that contemporary postcolonial studies recognize trauma as a complex phenomenon, extending beyond individual, acute events to encompass collective and chronic experiences. "Trauma can weaken individuals and communities, but it can also lead to a stronger sense of identity and renewed social cohesion."[19] Among those traumatic histories of subordinate groups that Visser wants to bring into the broader context of socially dominant groups are the experiences of racially differentiated women.

Pain and suffering are universal experiences, but the afterlife or memory of traumatic events differ for survivors according to their social position; women, ethnic or racial minorities, refugees, and people living in poverty are not afforded the same levels of understanding and protection that are granted to survivors with more social capital. The compounding impacts of gender and race for the women represented in this collection mean that their pain is too often overlooked in accounts of war and displacement. More importantly, it also reveals the ways in which their trauma is objectified or co-opted into larger national or religious narratives of suffering.[20] As the authors in this collection

---

[15] Ibid., 250.
[16] Ibid., 253.
[17] Ibid., 254.
[18] Ibid., 254.
[19] Ibid., 263.
[20] Although there is currently very little English-language scholarship on Arab and West Asian women's experiences of trauma, there is a growing body of research that addresses gendered pain in other postcolonial contexts. For instance, Zoë Norridge's Perceiving Pain in African Literature, Antjie Krog's There Was This Goat, and Pumla Gobodo-Madikizela's A Human Being Died that Night all explore specific forms of violence against women in the

have pointed out, non-Western women's pain is rarely allowed to exist. Instead, it is twisted into a symbolic representation of patriotic duty, sexual desire, or the object of masculine "protection." In these cases, any potential for individual resistance or recovery is overshadowed by the political exigency of a particular narrative. However, the impulse to resist narrative subsumption is still evident in women's testimonies of their individual traumas, and it is a social and political imperative to unearth their experiences and refute the symbolic potential that others attempt to impose upon them.

Numerous theorists, including Judith Herman, contend that psychoanalytic understandings of trauma, particularly those put forth by Freud and his followers, gradually veered away from reality. According to Herman, "psychoanalysis became a study of the internal vicissitudes of fantasy and desire, dissociated from the reality of experience."[21] However, Geoffrey Hartman offers a nuanced psychoanalytic elucidation of the "real," which proves particularly valuable in the ongoing debate and our exploration of literary and artistic representations of trauma and post-traumatic suffering within this collection.

Hartman employs Lacan's concept of the real to illustrate that Freud did not entirely disregard empirical reality; rather, he pointed to the existence of a distinct form of reality. Hartman explains that "the real is not the real, in the sense of a specific, identifiable thing or cause; however specific it may be, it is also a burning idea or its own 'wake' of desire." [22] In relation to the representation of trauma explored in this collection, the real can be found" within the world of 'death-feelings, lost objects, and drives." [23] This approach is particularly valuable in highlighting that the specific moment of "unmediated shock" and the subsequent inner turmoil, overflow of emotions, recurring imagery and memories, or the agonizing longing for the departed loved one is no less real than external, identifiable causes. In these instances, the real is simply that which eludes linguistic elaboration, even though its historical origins can be traced, and it can be diagnosed based on its physical symptoms. For instance, the intense desire for death experienced by a female victim of the Iran-Iraq war is explored in the first chapter in the wake of her excruciating pain.

Hartman asserts that this understanding of the real leads us towards literary theory, as "the disjunction between experiencing (phenomenal or empirical)

African context, while Kaiama L. Glover's A Regarded Self interrogates the narratives of women's pain and resistance in Caribbean literature and Urvashi Butalia's The Other Side of Silence covers the traumatic history of India's partition in 1947. For a more comprehensive and comparative analysis of women, literature, and trauma around the world, we recommend checking out Trauma and Literature, edited by J. Roger Kurtz.
[21] Herman, Trauma and Recovery, 14.
[22] Hartman, "On Traumatic Knowledge," 539.
[23] Ibid., 539.

and understanding (thoughtful naming, in which words replace things, or their images) is what figurative language expresses and explores." [24] Despite Dominick LaCapra's critique of their post-structuralist approach, he shares a common ground with Caruth and Hartman in emphasizing the disconcerting and irresolvable impact of trauma on the victim. This shared viewpoint makes their arguments deserving of attention, especially in the context of colonialism's wounds and the suffering endured by non-white populations.

In order to begin to understand the full impact of suffering in literary and artistic representation, trauma theory must account for both concepts of the Real: the deconstructionists' emphasis on the failure of language and the power of the unconscious in naming trauma, *and* the postcolonial trauma theorists' emphasis on the historical-material conditions that produce the context in which trauma occurs. When analyzed together, these two seemingly disparate approaches produce a more nuanced version of traumatic totality–one that begins to account for individual psychology and collective histories. The following chapters take both perspectives seriously, engaging with the histories of colonialism, racism, and sexism in order to make sense of individual experiences of loss and desire. While each chapter focuses on a unique case study or series of objects, they collectively demonstrate the importance of acknowledging the diversity of experiences and voices in representations of trauma throughout different historical and cultural contexts and offer forms of resistance to easy symbolic interpretation.

The first two chapters focus on the representation of women's experiences of war in contemporary art, which has been dominated by male perspectives, eclipsing women's accounts of their own experiences. The first chapter by Maryam Ghodrati delves into the embodiment of testimonies from the Iran-Iraq War, capturing both the institutional ecstasy felt by those in power and the individual agony endured by the survivors. Building upon Rothberg's concept of traumatic realism, Ghodrati specifically focuses on visual representations of trauma in the aftermath of the Iran-Iraq War, taking into account their gendered dimensions. She examines how these representations reveal the interconnectedness of bodies, state conventions, and national concerns, shedding light on the gendered consequences that arise in the wake of violence. By embracing a multidirectional memory and adopting a traumatic realist approach, this chapter explicitly challenges the tendency of postcolonial trauma theory to prioritize collective experiences and overlook individual narratives. According to Ghodrati, art acts as a challenge to dominant narratives of war and nation, inspiring critical engagement with women's attempts to reclaim their stories from subsumption into nationalist ideology.

---

[24] Ibid., 540.

Similarly, James Young's analysis of artistic depictions of women in the Holocaust (Chapter 2) emphasizes the need for gender-sensitive approaches to memory and experiences of trauma. However, unlike Ghodrati, Young's argument focuses on how art that represents women's experiences disregards or even negates the desires of its subjects. He points out that visual and literary depictions of Jewish women's suffering during the Holocaust often tend to objectify women's bodies and obfuscate their psychological pain and voices. Employing Susan Sontag's work on photography and pain alongside the large body of literature that explores gender and Holocaust memory, Young argues that the public gaze of photographers, curators, historians, and museumgoers continues to turn women into objects of memory, idealized casts of perfect suffering and victimization, and emblems of larger Jewish suffering during the Holocaust. The result of the interaction between artist, viewer, and subject means that even though women's pain is often held in high regard, it is also made a spectacle–converting the individual's suffering into cultural and even psychological objects full of symbolism.

The third and fourth chapters shift the focus away from visual art and focus instead on representations of Palestinian women's trauma in literature. These works explore how a retreat into the Lacanian concept of the Imaginary offers a sense of liberation, or at least resistance, to colonial frameworks of violence and control. Layla AlAmmar's chapter (Chapter 3) argues that the female protagonists of Ghada Samman's *Kawābīs Beirut* and Samar Yazbek's *Planet of Clay* react to the utter breakdown of their social realities by retreating into the fantasy-laden, visual field of the Imaginary. Both protagonists narrate their stories under conditions of escalating violence as the Lebanese Civil War and the Syrian Civil War, respectively, erupt around them. Consequently, they evince axiomatic aesthetics of trauma, such as compulsive repetitions and silence, which revert to Freudian understandings of trauma. However, by drawing on Jacques Lacan's register of orders, the analysis shifts from an individual, pathologizing view of the protagonists to the wider psychosocial implications of how the respective wars have ruptured the Symbolic and revealed the traumatic Real, which AlAmmar argues manifests as neopatriarchal hegemonic structures which continually generate war paradigms. In both narratives, a semiotic, pre-symbolic dimension allows the protagonists to articulate trauma in a way that eschews the violent discourse of men. However, despite finding some refuge in the Imaginary, both are ultimately made to confront the Symbolic. This reading of Samman and Yazbek's works challenges the "unspeakable" paradigm of trauma theory while simultaneously attending to individual experience and consciousness within systems of social hegemony.

Nora Parr, on the other hand, focuses her analysis in Chapter 4 on the relationship between individual trauma and the larger experience of Palestinians who have been displaced. She takes the position that the understanding of trauma cannot be universalized, but the language associated with it can be productively used–and manipulated–for decolonial purposes. Parr argues that Jabra Ibrahim Jabra's novel *The Search for Walid Masoud* rejects the "working through or sense" – making goals of trauma theory by introducing terms of psychoanalysis, creating a critical distance from them, and ultimately transforming the vocabulary of trauma to fashion a unique schema of meaning that is symbolically valuable and unique to a particular community of Palestinian emigrants in Baghdad. Parr claims that though the novel offers no explicit or universal definition of trauma and refuses to address whether or not it can be fully decolonized, Jabra's work does suggest that psychoanalysis and trauma theory can, and have been, re-deployed by postcolonial authors to resist Western influence and hegemony.

The fifth and final chapter returns to the issue of traumatic representation and witnessing by problematizing Benh Zeitlin's portrayal of the gendered and racialized messianic figure in his 2012 film *Beasts of the Southern Wild.* Concetta Principe argues that the putative Black savior fantasy on screen is riddled with the white American trauma that sustains America's racist history despite its hopeful message and seeming subversion of expectations. Using Lacan's understanding of the Real and Agamben's concept of the "messianic remnant," Principe asks the question: whose trauma is being represented? Like Young's claim that visual art has failed to fully represent Jewish women's traumatic experiences in the Holocaust, Principe argues that Zeitlin's film and Doris Betts' short story struggle to account for the racial trauma of Black Americans, ultimately projecting a fantasy that attempts to assuage the guilt and frustration of white Americans instead. Her framework begs the audience to think critically about the social and political impact of traumatic representation, rejecting a simplistic association between the experiences of a specific subject and the trauma of the community at large.

Taken together, these chapters engage with issues of universality and specificity; they show that there is not one easy way to strike a balance between deconstructivist ideas about trauma and postcolonial or pluralist approaches. The authors in this collection demonstrate the necessity of embracing a dynamic and diverse approach to the representation of trauma that makes marginalized survivors visible while also recognizing the complexities of gendered and racialized experiences of trauma. By analyzing marginalized representations of trauma, the work in this collection establishes connections and methods for reading trauma within (and against) both the deconstructivist and postcolonial paradigms of trauma theory. Connecting the values of postcolonial and deconstructionist trauma theory is of particular importance in a globalized world, where the legacies of colonialism continue to impact societies and cultures in complex ways–affecting individuals and communities. Rather than pitting them against one another, this volume presents diverse methods for how these approaches can inform and strengthen one another.

Bibliography

Balaev, Michelle. *Contemporary Approaches in Literary Trauma Theory.* New York: Palgrave Macmillan, 2014.

Caruth, Cathy. *Unclaimed Experience: Trauma, Narrative, and History.* Baltimore: Johns Hopkins University Press, 1996.

Hartman, Geoffrey H. "On Traumatic Knowledge and Literary Studies." *New Literary History* 26, no. 3, 1995: 537–563.

Herman, Judith. *Trauma and Recovery: The Aftermath of Violence—From Domestic Abuse to Political Terror.* New York: Basic Books, 1997.

Kleinman, Arthur. *The Illness Narratives: Suffering, Healing, and the Human Condition.* New York: Basic Books, 1989.

Scarry, Elaine. *The Body in Pain: The Making and Unmaking of the World.* New York: Oxford University Press, 1985.

Vickroy, Laurie. *Trauma and Survival in Contemporary Fiction.* Charlottesville: University of Virginia Press, 2002.

Visser, Irene. "Decolonizing Trauma Theory; Retrospect and Prospects." *Humanities* 4, no. 2, 2015: 250–265.

Further Reading

Adorno, Theodor W. (auth.) and Robert Hullot-Kentor (ed. and trans.). *Aesthetic Theory.* Minneapolis: University of Minnesota Press, 1998.

Adorno, Theodor W. (auth.) and E.F.N. Jephcott (trans.). *Minima Moralia: Reflections from Damaged Life.* New York: Verso, 2020.

LaCapra, Dominick. *Writing History, Writing Trauma.* Baltimore: Johns Hopkins University Press, 2001.

Chapter 1

Embodied Testimonies: Institutional Ecstasy, Individual Agony, and Visual Representation of the Body at War

Maryam Ghodrati

University of Massachusetts Amherst

Abstract

This chapter delves into the embodiment of testimonies from the Iran-Iraq War, capturing both the institutional ecstasy felt by those in power and the individual agony endured by the survivors. It explores the representation of this war, acknowledging the limitations of language in conveying the profound depths of suffering. Building upon Rothberg's concept of traumatic realism, the chapter specifically focuses on visual representations of trauma in the aftermath of the Iran-Iraq War, taking into account their gendered dimensions. It examines how these representations reveal the interconnectedness of bodies, state conventions, and national concerns, shedding light on the oppressive consequences that often arise. By embracing a multidirectional memory and adopting a traumatic realist approach, this section challenges prevailing postcolonial trauma theory, which tends to prioritize collective experiences and overlook individual narratives. It advocates for a deconstructive perspective that uncovers the universality of human experiences under extreme conditions.

Keywords: trauma, survival, embodiment, testimonies, Iran-Iraq War, traumatic realism, power dynamics, state conventions, national concerns, multidirectional memory, postcolonial trauma theory, collective vs. individual experience, deconstructive approach, universality of human experience

* * *

The key to the survivor experience, the basis for all survivor themes, is the imprint of death.[1]

---

[1] Robert Jay Lifton, *Death in Life* (Chapel Hill: University of North Carolina Press, 1991), 480.

> At the heart of traumatic narrative there is a kind of double telling, the
> oscillation between a crisis of death and the correlative crisis of life;
> between the story of the unbearable nature of an event and the story of
> the unbearable nature of its survival.[2]

"I want to die." These four words made up the entire text message I was sent by
a woman in her early thirties from Western Iran, a woman who was contaminated
by the chemical bombardment of her village when she was two years old. She
was left behind in the chaos as villagers perished or fled for their lives during
the Iran-Iraq War, which lasted from 1980 until 1988. The sentence lay there,
bare, simple, naked in front of my eyes, for a few long minutes as I struggled to
respond. Then came a close-up selfie of her face all swollen, turned purple and
blue, soaked by the tears running down her cheeks as she lay helplessly, her
head on a pillow. It was yet another flare-up, the result of damage to her lungs
from chemical exposure during the war. Gasping for air, the body's demand for
oxygen sent excruciating pain all over her body, an experience that would be
repeated throughout her life, resulting in hospitalization each time. What did
the few words of her text message have to do with what was actually happening
in her body and psyche? How did they describe her pain, except by making it
inescapable, wordless, and less sharable, as if death itself was the only
communicable meaning, the only escape from her sense of defeat, confronted
with the clutching hands of her suffering and the impossibility of having any
control over the pain? Her pain and suffering became a self-referential and self-
destructive force, an atemporal experience analogous to nothingness, outside
of the boundaries of reality, a devouring abyss. In part, perhaps her desire for
"death" came from her inability to endure and to narrativize the experience of
the extreme, to materialize it, to identify a point of comparison. This desire
prompted her to pronounce her subjectivity, her own existence. The "I" who
had demanded "death" – the forgotten subject hanging on the verge of death –
became visible, claiming agency over her isolated suffering. Had it not been for
the image she shared in that moment, her suffering would have remained a
secret, her demand for death an uncertain, untethered, abstract form of
desolation. With her ambiguous statement and with a sense of urgency, she
tried to share her unspeakable suffering, while "I," as the reader, remained in
doubt, unable to feel that same experience. Nothing happened in my body
except the vague throbbing of empathy and sorrow that swiftly passed through
my mind and heart.

This woman's plea for death, rooted in her struggle to convey the true nature
of her pain beyond mere words, resonates with the intellectual linguistic struggle

---

[2] Cathy Caruth, *Unclaimed Experience: Trauma, Narrative, and History* (Baltimore: Johns
Hopkins University Press, 1996), 7.

of Siegfried Sassoon throughout *Sherston's Progress* (1936) in his observation of the limitations of language in capturing the essence of suffering. Both this ordinary woman and the soldier-poet Sassoon confront the ineffable nature of trauma, which eludes simple descriptions and resists easy understanding. In *Sherston's Progress*, Siegfried Sassoon has written perhaps one of the most comprehensive statements about the post-traumatic consequences of war. As a soldier in World War I who was treated for shell shock, Sassoon artfully reveals the long-lasting psychological effects of exposure to traumatic events and their effect on the physical body, as well as the linguistic and communicative limitations and existential views of survivors of war:

> Shell-shock. How many a brief bombardment had its long-delayed after-effect in the minds of these survivors, many of whom had looked at their companions and laughed while the inferno did its best to destroy them. Not then was their evil hour, but now; now, in the sweating, suffocation of nightmare, in paralysis of limbs, in the stammering of dislocated speech. Worst of all, in the disintegration of those qualities through which they had been so gallant and selfless and uncomplaining – this, in the finer types of men, was the unspeakable tragedy of shell shock.[3]

Sassoon's revelatory vision came about long before research on traumatic disorders entered the public consciousness. During and after the end of World War I, shell-shocked soldiers were treated with repetitive and brutal electric shocks in order to restore their functionality and send them back to the frontlines. Hypnosis was another (supposedly) restorative treatment used to revitalize a soldier's memory and self-control. Those who showed signs of what today we would call PTSD were labeled as "morally invalid" and were court-martialed for expressing their concerns about the symptoms of post-traumatic stress. Sassoon's writings revealed the "disintegration" of the human subject and the "unspeakable tragedy of shell shock" decades before the trauma theories of the 1990s appeared. Sassoon's work asserted the nature of the unspeakability, incomprehensibility, and uncertainty of traumatic experience. The ordinary suffering subject was and is, particularly in the case of the civilian survivor, fully aware of the dismantling effects of suffering and its imposing limitations on language. The expressions of anguish and trauma conveyed by both the female victim of the Iran-Iraq War and the male perspective from Sassoon's autofictional diary underscore the challenges inherent in articulating the profound depths of suffering in the aftermath of conflict. These two individuals, despite their starkly different socio-political contexts and their

---

[3] Siegfried Sassoon, *The Complete Memoirs of George Sherston* (Chicago: World Book Inc., 1940) 557.

separation by time and space, share a common struggle in attempting to communicate the magnitude of their experiences.

The mainstream trauma theory of the 1990s, developed by Caruth, Felman, and Hartman and centering on unspeakability, has faced criticism from postcolonial scholars such as Visser, Balaev, and Craps. They argue that this theory fails to address the specific trauma experienced in the colonial world and instead adopts a deconstructivist approach that psychologizes traumatic experiences. Visser has called for a decolonized trauma theory that includes non-Western and non-European experiences, such as racism, colonial violence, and the everyday suffering of marginalized groups. Among the scholars on trauma theory, Michael Rothberg occupies a unique position that bridges the gap between the opposing approaches of postcolonial and deconstructive trauma theory. Rothberg, without denying the unspeakable nature of traumatic experience and its temporal and psychological dimensions, advocates for a more comprehensive approach to trauma, proposing a comparative examination of different traumatic histories and their representations. Even though he has been often quoted by postcolonial scholars in isolation to advocate for reconceiving trauma "as collective, spatial, and material (instead of individual, temporal, and linguistic)"[4] to emphasize the urgency of decolonizing trauma theory, Rothberg also goes on to build upon Caruthian theory and pose the problem differently from most scholars. He suggests that

> Instead of focusing criticism on the supposed "whiteness" of trauma studies' subjects, we might want to say that as long as trauma studies forego comparative study and remains tied to a narrow Eurocentric framework, it distorts the histories it addresses (such as the Holocaust) and threatens to reproduce the very Eurocentrism that lies behind those histories. [...] The question of whiteness leads to a second, equally important point. In addition to imposing an anachronistic racial categorization, the attribution of "white Westerners" also risks reproducing a notion of a homogenous "West" that stays within the terms of the dominant framework. What is the "West," and why would we want to evoke this highly ideological and Eurocentric concept? I mean this question quite seriously. Not only is the referent of the "West" highly elusive, but the use of the concept ends up confirming the racialized framework it seeks to mark and displace.[5]

In his analysis of Andre Schwarz-Bart's novel *A Woman Named Solitude* (*La mulâtresse Solitude*, 1972), Rothberg advocates for the use of "anachronism" and "anatopism" to represent multiple traumatic legacies. Through the use of

---

[4] Michael Rothberg, "Decolonizing Trauma Studies: A Response," *Studies in the Novel* 40, no. 1-2 (2008): 228.
[5] Ibid., 227-8.

these literary techniques, Schwarz-Bart's tale of transatlantic slavery connects the historical contexts of the Caribbean and the Warsaw Ghetto. This approach brings together the Holocaust, slavery, and colonialism as interconnected histories in what Rothberg terms "multidirectional memory."[6]

This chapter aims to bridge Caruthian trauma theory and postcolonial trauma theory by utilizing Rothberg's concept of traumatic realism. Focusing on visual representations of trauma and their gendered dimensions in the aftermath of the Iran-Iraq War, this research delves into the connection between bodies, state conventions, and national concerns, revealing the oppressive outcomes that often result. Drawing from Rothberg's insights, it explores multidirectional memory and traumatic realism to deepen understanding and responses to specific traumas. By drawing attention to the individual's unspeakable and invisible experiences of suffering as the basis for collective and socio-political engagement, this chapter challenges established postcolonial trauma theory, which often overemphasizes the collectivity of traumatic experience and subsumes individual stories under ideological notions of nationalism and self-determination. To achieve this goal, the chapter advocates for embracing a deconstructionist approach to the universality of human experience under extreme conditions in which the human body is at its most vulnerable. By amplifying survivors' voices and emphasizing a profound focus on gendered experiences, this research aims to foster integration between cultures and reassess the prevailing event-based model of trauma to encompass ongoing forms of traumatizing violence. Ultimately, it seeks to retell the historical past by exploring its aftermath and countering mystified and theologized narratives.

From Crucifixion to Mutilation: The Dismantled Western and European Body in the Aftermath of War

In 2003, decades after its creation, the reproduction of Picasso's *Guernica* hanging in the lobby of the United Nations Security Council in New York was covered with a blue curtain when then Secretary of Defense Colin Powell addressed the UN just before the planned bombing of Baghdad.[7] This act of censorship revealed not only the fundamental contradictions inherent to the politics of warfare and human values but also the fear of the immense moral and ethical influence that this iconic painting might have had on viewers during a time when the US was embarking on an imperial mission in Iraq. Politicians knew that the painting, with its depictions of mutilated and shrieking men,

---

[6] Michael Rothberg, *Multidirectional Memory: Remembering the Holocaust in an Age of Decolonization* (Redwood City: Stanford University Press, 2009).

[7] Maureen Dowd, "Powell Without Picasso," *The New York Times*, published 5 February 2003, https://www.nytimes.com/2003/02/05/opinion/powell-without-picasso.html.

women, children, and animals alike, had the power to make apparent the contradictions between the language of imperial power and Picasso's visual assertion of traumatic suffering.

Years later, in his 2015 book *War is Beautiful*, David Shields compiled a series of war photographs that appeared on the front page of *The New York Times* from the invasion of Afghanistan in 2001 and Iraq in 2003. The book is the result of his "enchanted and infuriated" state of mind when confronted with those images. According to Shields, the *Times* "uses its front-page war photographs to convey that a chaotic world is ultimately under control, encased within amber. In so doing, the paper of record promotes its institutional power as protector/curator of death-dealing democracy." "This," he writes, "is why I no longer read *The New York Times*."[8] Shields's disillusionment with the newspaper reflects his recognition of the manipulation and distortion of visual representations of conflict. The connection between Shields's disillusionment with *The New York Times'* representation of war and the covering of *Guernica* lies in their shared emphasis on the manipulation and distortion of visual representations of conflict by powerful institutions. Shields's book, *War is Beautiful*, critiques *The New York Times* for using front-page war photographs that convey a sense of control and stability, promoting the newspaper's institutional power as a curator of war imagery.

Together, these instances highlight the significance of visual art and photography as mediums that have the potential to challenge dominant narratives. By examining these acts of censorship and manipulation, we are prompted to question the role of the media, the politics of warfare, and the ethical implications of visual storytelling in the context of conflict. Ultimately, they emphasize the disjunction between the bystander and the individual caught in the violence of war, inviting the audience to critically engage with the relationship between power, representation, and the human experience of violence.

The fate that befell Picasso's *Guernica* in the UN lobby was not an isolated incident, as numerous other artists, such as Otto Dix, have experienced similar censorship in times of imperialist warfare. Dix, who actively served in WWI and received a medal of honor for his service, was haunted by its gruesome sights, which inspired his famous portfolio of fifty etchings called *The War*[9]. Despite his accolades, Dix was still labeled a "degenerate" artist by fascist authorities under the Third Reich, and his 1923 triptych painting *The Trench*[10] was veiled

---

[8] David Shields, *War is Beautiful: The New York Times Pictorial Guide to the Glamour of Armed Conflict* (New York: PowerHouse Books, 2015), 7-9.

[9] In the original German: *Der Krieg*

[10] In the original German: *Der Schützengraben*

behind a curtain and removed from the Wallraf-Richartz Museum[11]. Dix's fascination with human decay and grotesque imagery in his works demonstrate war's horrible consequences, which destroy and annihilate. The grotesque emptiness of suffering depicted by Dix stands in direct contrast to the mainstream, overwhelmingly Christian depictions of suffering found in earlier artwork of death.[12] In the new modern world, forever changed by WWI, the human body in pain dismantled all romantic idealization of compassion and redemption presented by the Crucifixion of Christ. His paintings depict the absurd "nothingness" that defines death in battle, paralleling Goya's *The Disasters of War* [13] series. Dix's paintings show the human subject as a target of indignity and humiliation, exemplified in *The Wounded Man* and *House Destroyed by Aircraft Bombs*. The works of Picasso, Goya, and Dix, though set in different historical and cultural contexts, all demonstrate the disintegration and humiliation of the human subject in times of war.

Whether abstract, realist, or surrealist,[14] artwork that behaves like a "whistle-blower," to use the moral philosopher Jonathan Glover's term, is not simply a passive sign or reference to a particular history or a certain ideology. Art has the power and agency to bring to life a certain kind of thought, to change and challenge normalizing conventions. It can move people "to witness without speaking and to make it difficult to sustain ignorance or innocence in the face of suffering."[15] The censorship that artists like Picasso and Dix were subjected to reveals a pervasive fear that art can become a "civilizing force that erases national boundaries and strengthens human solidarity."[16] Humans and animals, civilians and warriors alike, are all slaughtered in *Guernica* (Figure 1.1), exposed within a closed frame of darkness that offers no escape, no beacon of hope or redemption. Picasso's *Guernica*, like Goya's *Disasters* series, is devoid of light. Like Dix, for Picasso, both spirituality and conventional religion turn out to be pointless in the chaos of war. *Guernica* represents his skepticism towards

---

[11] Dennis Crockett, "The Most Famous Painting of the 'Golden Twenties'? Otto Dix and the Trench Affair," *Art Journal* 51, no. 1 (1992): 79.

[12] Dix's triptych has been compared with The Isenheim Altarpiece, sculpted and painted by Germans Nikolaus of Haguenau and Matthias Grünewald in 1512–1516, as well as *The Descent from the Cross*, a triptych painting by Peter Paul Rubens 1612–1614.

[13] In the original Spanish: *Los Desastres de la Guerra*.

[14] See Salvador Dalí's *Boiled Beans* (1936), an example of Soft Construction in which individuals in the Spanish Civil War are depicted with contorted limbs and agonized expressions.

[15] David Campbel quoted in Catherine Craven, "How the Visual Arts Can Further the Cause of Human Rights," *E-International Relations*, published 27 October 2011, https://www.e-ir.info/2011/10/27/the-visual-arts-and-the-cause-of-human-rights-in-dealing-with-suffering-and-trauma/#google_vignette.

[16] Guerin and Hallas in Craven, "How the Visual Arts…"

Christian themes such as iconography, martyrdom, and redemption. It subverts the traditional Christian imagery where divine light emanates from above, transforming it into a foreboding light resembling a vigilant eye that has brought chaos and death. Instead of the peaceful and hopeful dove symbolizing freedom, there is a screaming dove, its beak wide open in distress. The heroic figure or warrior, typically portrayed triumphantly, now lies defeated with a shattered sword in a mutilated hand. The iconic image of the Virgin Mary from the Pietà, known for its gentle contours, is reimagined as a tormented mother with sharp, piercing edges. Unlike Mary, this mother emits a scream, her tongue resembling a sword.[17] This portrayal of the extreme vulnerability of all living beings in the face of war's brutality transcends any specific ideology. Guernica becomes a universal representation of anguish, pain, and suffering, symbolizing all bombed cities and their collective suffering.[18] (Figure 1.1, *Guernica*)

Figure 1.1 *Guernica*. "Mural del *Guernica* de Picasso" (Mosaical Reproduction of *Guernica* by Pablo Picasso, 1937, oil painting), mosaic tiles, Guernica, Spain.

Over a century earlier, Francisco Goya, disillusioned with the promises of the Enlightenment, created the *Disasters of War* series. Produced between 1810 and 1820, the series of 82 prints depicts the futility of human struggle against human brutality. Although Goya was called upon to record the "glorious exploits" during the siege of Saragossa by Napoleon's army, he saw nothing glorious in the chaotic

---

[17] Robert Rosenblum, "Picasso's Disasters of War: The Art of Blasphemy," in *Picasso and the War Years, 1937-1945*, ed. Pablo Picasso (London: Thames and Hudson, 1998), 46-48.
[18] According to Catherine Craven, *Guernica* was described in this way by José Camón Aznar in the first Spanish monograph on Picasso, *Picasso y la Escuela Española* (1951).

violence.[19] *The Disasters of War* series reveals the limitations of human imagination in comprehending the experiences of others. Goya does not take sides with either party to the conflict; rather, his drawings are detached and reflective. Civilians are the central, unwitting targets of the siege's brutality, yet they are not portrayed as heroes. They are shown simultaneously as victims of indignity and humiliation but equally cruel and bloodthirsty. Like *Guernica*, Goya's etchings are devoid of color, and, as Susan Sontag observes, he "eliminates all the trappings of the spectacular, the landscape becomes an atmosphere, a darkness barely sketched in. War is not a spectacle."[20] *The Disasters of War* series was not displayed in public; it was found and published posthumously in 1863. Goya's vision was considered too dark by Spanish authorities, who sought to maintain their legitimacy by representing the world under their reign as a safe place.

The experience of pain, suffering, and death form a fundamental common ground shared by all humans. However, its representation in art is often influenced by the social, political, and cultural context in which it is created. The raw emotions associated with suffering and the challenges of effectively conveying those experiences are frequently suppressed to uphold dominant narratives. However, artworks like *The Disasters of War* series and *Guernica* disrupt this trend of censorship by exposing the horrors of war and their profound impact on civilians and soldiers alike. These powerful creations dismantle the glorification of war perpetuated by those in power, depicting the human subject as a target of indignity and humiliation. Through their vision, the artists compel society to confront the stark reality of war and the devastating toll it takes on humanity.

Pietà and the Crucified Body in the Art of the Islamic Republic

The devastation of warfare depicted by these European artists is equally found in the non-Western world. The Iran-Iraq War (1980-1988) took place in the context of the Islamic Revolution of 1979, which emerged partly as a response to years of Euro-Western exploitation and interference in Iran and established the nation as the Islamic Republic of Iran. The conflict escalated when, in 1980, the Iraqi army invaded the Iranian border in the south, leading to a deadly war supported by various Euro-Western powers. The war resembled World War I in its tactics, including the use of chemical weapons such as mustard gas by Iraq against Iranian troops, civilians, and Iraqi Kurds. Despite confirmation by the UN Security Council of Iraq's use of chemical weapons, the international

---

[19] Gassier et al, The Life and Complete Works, 217.
[20] Susan Sontag, Regarding the Pain of Others (New York: Farrar, Straus, and Giroux, 2003), 44.

community remained largely silent.[21] The war, known within Iran as the Imposed War or the Holy Defense, lasted for eight years and resulted in over a million deaths and casualties.

During the Iran-Iraq War, the dominant artistic genre in Iran, known as the Art of Revolution, Art of Resistance, and Art of Sacred Defense, utilized symbolic representation to establish a spiritual meaning for the pain and suffering endured by the nation. This approach emphasized the collective sacrifice for a greater cause, contrasting with Western perspectives that focused on the material reality of dismembered bodies and bloodshed. The Islamic Republic's philosophy, as reflected in the views of Morteza Goodarzi Dibaj, the director of Iran's Howze Honari Visual Art Center, challenged the Western philosophy of individualism and criticized its limited focus on the psychological aspect of trauma. "War is beautiful for us," said Dibja. "Westerners see only the surface, the dismembered bodies, bloodshed, and absurdity of death. We see the world differently. We see the beauty of sacrifice for a great cause. War was imposed on us, and we resisted to our last drop of blood. Pain and suffering are not important for us."

Consequently, in the aftermath of the Islamic revolution and the Iran-Iraq War, death took on symbolic significance, intertwined with the concept of eternal life as a means of coping with the suffering and misery endured by the Iranian people. Both men and women played significant roles during the war, but both genders were reduced to mere symbols to represent ideas. Women's bodies were perceived and understood as vehicles of nurturing and fortitude, with their role as mothers and caregivers seen as vital in shaping the future generation of defenders. The body, in this case, becomes a site of knowledge and meaning, as the act of nurturing and raising children is imbued with significance for the nation's survival and resilience. Men became revered symbols of resistance against the perceived oppressive forces of the imperial world, drawing parallels to the martyrdom of Imam Hossein in Karbala.

To create a hegemonic narrative, obliged by Khomeini's ideals of a utopian society, Iranian filmmakers embraced the new revolutionary ideologies. They embarked on the mass production of propaganda films, known as "Cinema for Sacred Defense." These films were carefully controlled by the Islamic Republic and aimed to sanctify the war by presenting it through moral and religious imperatives. Similarly, literature and visual art became synonymous with the

---

[21] Extensive use of Chemical Weapons in the 20th century occurred in the Iran-Iraq conflict, facilitated by technical assistance from the European and U.S. private sector. The administrations of George H. W. Bush and Ronald Reagan provided substantial support to Iraq's chemical and biological weapons programs. For more, see Haines, D. D., and S. C. Fox. "Acute and Long-Term Impact of Chemical Weapons: Lessons from the Iran-Iraq War." *Forensic Science Review* 26, no. 2 (July 2014): 97–114.

cultural productions of the Iran-Iraq War. However, despite the enduring physical and psychological consequences suffered by a significant number of Iranians even decades after the war, the visual art representing these effects avoids portraying the true extent of the suffering. Instead, the post-revolutionary establishment has promoted an aesthetic of religious revival and nationalist identity while marginalizing the post-traumatic and mutilated bodies that deviate from the idealized revolutionary narrative. This dynamic reflects a propagandist and politically motivated subjugation of the human body, where the reality of suffering is overshadowed by the promotion of religious and nationalistic ideals. Post-traumatic bodies, which bear the physical and psychological scars of war, are rendered marginalized and excluded from the narrative of revolution and war unless they adhere to the holiness of revolution.

Like the Holocaust or the Shoah (names created to describe the specificity of the extermination of Jews in Europe), the war against Iran was branded as a Holy War and Sacred Defense.[22] Within the field of Holocaust studies, a deliberate distinction has been made between sacred and secularized depictions of this significant historical event, with the former aligning with a modernist aesthetic and the latter with a postmodern aesthetic.[23] In the discourse of "modern and sacralization," Elie Wiesel assigns a "religious significance to the events of the Holocaust," seeing it as "equal to the revelation at Sinai." Wiesel has even suggested that "attempts to desanctify or demystify the Holocaust are subtle forms of anti-Semitism."[24] In contrast, Rothberg relates the unknowable nature of this event, i.e., the desacralization of the Holocaust, to the postmodern tendency to place it in "relation to the circumstances of its representation in the present, eschewing the stance of an objective observer who registers timeless truth."[25] He employs this postmodern approach to examine any historical event that has been connected to religious connotations, and the Iran-Iraq war is undeniably one such event.

---

[22] In the case of Iran, war has been named by the official discourse as Jang-e Eslam va Kofr (The Battle of Islam Against Infidelity), Emtehan-e Elahi (the Devine Test) Nabard-e Hagh Alayh-e Batel (The battle of Right against Wrong) and Defa-e Moghaddas (the Holy or Sacred Defense). See Khorrami, Mohammad Mehdi. "Narratives of Silence: Persian Fiction of the 1980-1988 Iran-Iraq War." *In Moments of Silence: Authenticity in the Cultural Expressions of the Iran-Iraq War, 1980-1988*: 217-235. Edited by Arta Khakpour et al. New York: New York University Press, 2016, pp. 217–235.

[23] Michael Rothberg, *Traumatic Realism: The Demands of Holocaust Representation* (Minneapolis: University of Minnesota Press, 2000), 5.

[24] Elie Wiesel quoted in Rothberg, *Traumatic Realism*, 5.

[25] Dora Apel, *Memory Effects: The Holocaust and the Art of Secondary Witnessing* (New Brunswick: Rutgers University Press, 2002), 7.

The notion of the "Sacred Defense" in the context of the Iran-Iraq War, like the Holocaust, points to its already mystified and sacralized nature. This tendency almost immediately obliterates any postmodern understanding of the historical catastrophe and its aftermath. Naming this history as "sacred" places it outside the boundaries of analysis and criticism; consequently, any attempt at more secular ways of understanding is perceived as analogous to corruption and disbelief in God and the afterlife, thus blocking any attempt at alternative representations of post-traumatic culture in Iran. Sacralizing the war efforts and making martyrs of its victims has created a visual parallel to the theme in Christian art of depicting the death of Jesus – the anti-Western art of the Sacred Defense centers around the parallel glorification of the crucified body of the martyr. Even in death, soldiers are segregated as martyrs in their graveyards, which are given titles such as "The Flower Garden of Martyrs" or "Martyr's Paradise."[26] These numerous memorials also supplement the sacralization that surrounds the nature of this war and anything related to it, as if the event has only one story to tell and the story that it tells has only one meaning. The Iran-Iraq War, like many other wars before and since, was deemed to be a conflict between good and evil, between the corrupt and the righteous; thus, the facts of imperial and colonial politics, as well as the politics of resistance and defense, produced a national identity that was from another dimension, and the historical and material reality, nevertheless, lent itself to immaterial meaning.

Khomeini's revolutionary movement championed the cause of the dispossessed and oppressed. It used Shia ideology and religious symbolism "in elevating the revolution to a moral and spiritual battle against an infidel."[27] He held the West responsible for Iran's internal problems and saw Dr. Ali Shariati (1933-1977), a leading anti-colonial theorist in Iran, and his discourse on revolutionary Shiism, and proclaimed Islam on the side of the mustazafin, the dispossessed, and against exploiters and imperialists.[28] As an "ideologue of the Iranian revolution," Shariati, a Sorbonne-educated leftist sociologist who became a renowned scholar of struggle in the modern Middle East, introduced the theory of struggle between oppressors and the oppressed. Heavily influenced by the West Indian psychoanalyst and social philosopher from the French colony of Martinique, Frantz Fanon (1925-1961),[29] Shariati justified Shiite jihad against

---

[26] Shahla Talebi, "From the Light of the Eyes to the Eyes of the Power: State and Dissident Martyrs in Post-Revolutionary Iran," *Visual Anthropology* 25, no. i-ii (2012): 128.
[27] Eric Egan, *The Films of Makhmalbaf: Cinema, Politics & Culture in Iran* (Washington, D.C.: Mage Publishers, 2005), 57.
[28] See Abrahamian, Ervand. *Iran Between Two Revolutions*. Princeton: Princeton University Press, 1982.
[29] Shariati translated Fanon's writings into Persian in the 1960s, introducing his influential analysis of colonialism's impact on racial consciousness. Fanon's multidisciplinary approach

the "Great Satan," an epithet referring to the United States in Iran following the revolution.[30] Islam and Shiite identity in the colonial and imperial context became an effective tool of resistance that gave a distinct identity to revolutionaries and the populace, a national pride, and a sense of unity in order to overcome Euro-Western puppetry and occupation. For the revolutionary Iranian nation that has based its foundation on a rhetoric of independence from imperial powers, the "I" of the individual always melts into the "we" of a nation, drawing influence from Frantz Fanon, himself influenced by Aimé Césaire, another leading intellectual of the anti-colonial movement. Both Césaire and Fanon put forward the idea of a national literature and a national culture, acknowledging the importance of cultural nationalism, culminating in the development of national awareness. Through Dr. Ali Shariati's translating, teaching, and preaching to the masses in Iran, Fanonian theories of self-creation and national liberation helped shape the Iranian revolution, especially the Fanonian idea of an anti-colonial self-creation of a "new man." However, his model of a "new man" in the process of self-creation was distinct from Fanon, who rejected religion as a basis for "anticolonial selfhood."[31]

In contrast, Shariati, who has been named "the Fanon of the Islamic Revolution,"[32] highlighted the significance of revisiting the religious narrative of Shiism as a powerful means of opposing imperialism, ultimately leading to the triumph of the Islamic Revolution. "The mobilization of the masses," asserts Fanon, "when it arises out of the war of liberation, introduces into each man's consciousness the ideas of a common cause, of a national destiny, and of a collective history."[33] Shariati advocated for the integration of collective religious history into the consciousness of the masses, emphasizing the importance of Hossein as a role model and martyrdom as a way of life that Muslim society should adopt in its process of reconstructing the self, specifically in its anti-colonial and anti-imperial endeavors.

---

encompassed psychoanalysis, phenomenology, existentialism, and Negritude theory, shedding light on the extensive psychosocial repercussions of colonialism on the colonized.
[30] See Apolinar, Lydia. "Ali Shariati: Ideologue of the Iranian Revolution." Cosmonaut, Inc. 29 November 2019. https://cosmonaut.blog/2019/11/29/ali-shariati-ideologue-of-the-iranian-revolution/.
[31] Frantz Fanon 's Contribution to Postcolonial Criticism by Nasrullah Mambrol on April 7, 2016.
[32] Ervand Abrahamian, qtd. in Arash Davari, "A Return to Which Self?: 'Ali Shari' Ati and Frantz Fanon on the Political Ethics of Insurrectionary Violence," *Comparative Studies of South Asia* 34, no. 1 (2014): 86.
[33] Frantz Fanon (auth.) and Richard Philcox (trans.), *The Wretched of the Earth* (New York: Grove Press, 1977), 47.

Following the revolution, Iranian artists embarked on an anti-imperialist struggle to reconstruct their identity and subjectivity amidst the remnants of a tragic historical backdrop. Consequently, numerous Iranian paintings created during and after the Iran-Iraq War merge the revolutionary Shiite identity of these artists with the present moment. The transcendental powers of patience, sacrifice, belief, and resistance are interwoven into the form, color, and content of Iranian post-revolutionary painting that signifies a non-materialist conception of the world. Renowned contemporary painters like Kazem Chalipa (1958-), often referred to as the "artist of the revolution," portrayed modern soldiers as the martyrs of the Battle of Karbala in 680 AD. This historic battle saw the martyrdom of Hossein, the third Shiite Imam, his brothers, sons, and seventy-two followers, who valiantly opposed the oppressive forces. Complementing these works that present symbolic death in holy battle, women are similarly portrayed as the ideal object with which to symbolize anti-Western ideology. They were depicted as iconic figures of patience and sacrifice, intended to present the nation as one strong, unbending force against the Satanic forces of the world.[34] The ideological pressure on women as national symbols centered around their response to the violence and loss of war. Janet Afary's study of war widows reveals that the Islamic State often persuaded women that the loss of their sons as martyrs was cause not for grief but for celebration and assured them that they gained greater recognition in the eyes of the almighty as a result.[35] Kazem Chalipa's *Sacrifice* (1981), *Resistance* (1983), and *Desert* (1984), with their repetitive themes and styles, are exemplary images of the ideal woman in times of revolution and war. These women mourn their losses with dignity and stoic patience as they sacrifice their sons to the path of God in order to save humanity without doubting their holy mission.

The prevailing narrative upholds the belief that women, like men, played a crucial role during times of war – not by fighting in battle but by symbolically embodying national values and supporting their men on the front lines. Drawing inspiration from the story of Zeinab, Imam Hossein's sister in the battle of Karbala, these women are seen as the inheritors of her courageous spirit. Despite witnessing the brutality and tragedy of war, Zeinab defiantly stands against corrupt authority, responding to inquiries about her experience by stating, "I saw nothing but beauty." Chalipa's painting, *Sacrifice* (Figure 1.2),

---

[34] *In Staging a Revolution: The Art of Persuasion in the Islamic Republic of Iran,* Peter Chelkowski and Hamid Dabashi examine the ideological and propagandist machinery of visual production in Iran in the words of Ayatollah Khomeini, the charismatic leader of the Revolution, revolutionary posters, banners, murals, graffiti, songs, and oratorios, that was mobilized by the leading figures of the revolutionary movement.
[35] Janet Afary, *Sexual Politics in Modern Iran* (New York: Cambridge University Press, 2009), 300.

follows this narrative of Zeinab, portraying beauty amidst war, destruction, and mutilation. In the painting, vibrant colors beckon the viewer into a world of beautiful combat. The divine light shines from the top center, casting its glow upon the historical figures dressed in white shrouds, standing in reverence to Imam Hossein. Occupying the middle center is Imam Hossein himself, holding the Holy Quran close to his heart and wielding a sword upright. The upper half of the painting, with its bluish-white hues, connects the historic battle of Karbala with the lower half's depiction of the Iran-Iraq war, which is depicted in red.

At the center-right, beneath Imam Hossein, stands the devoted woman, representing the epitome of Islamic femininity. She nurtures martyrdom, supports the selfless march of her sons, and tenderly holds a headless body as an offering. Her expression is solemn, her closed eyes turning inward as her skin blends with the surrounding colors. Nearby, a dead soldier's body transforms into a tulip, a symbol of martyrdom in Iranian Shi'i iconography, as his mother cradles him in a pose reminiscent of the Christian Pietà. To her right, a row of tulips represents the embryonic soldiers, while on her left, they have grown into adult soldiers, willingly marching toward the battlefield and their deaths. The symmetrical arrangement and transformation of subjects symbolize the continuous cycle of martyrdom and the everlasting unity of Shiite historical identity and revolutionary ideology. This portrayal reflects a chronological timeline of war and death; each event imbued with a specific meaning and purpose. It emphasizes the interconnectedness of past and present, the endurance of martyrdom's culture, and the profound unity within Shiite history and revolutionary ideals.[36]

In Chalipa's *Resistance* (Figure 1.3), a red brushstroke bleeds like a wound into the yellow wheat fields of the motherland, then into the orange of the sun on the horizon. The soldiers who have risen in ghostly shapes from the land march upright to leave the woman and the child at the center and the foreground of the frame to defend their dignity and identity. The color of their ethereal march behind the woman blends into the woman's surrealist, Dalí-esque hand. The destruction of the land is only symbolically present in the vibrant colors and her large hands, which represent her extraordinary endurance and strength. Her closed eyes, similar to the eyes of the woman in *Sacrifice*, turn her agony inward. Chalipa avoids enabling eye contact between his subjects and the viewer, emphasizing the spiritual experience of war as opposed to the material reality of striving and exposure to loss and pain. In *Desert* (Figure 1.4), the center of focus as in *Sacrifice* and *Resistance*, is again a woman with closed eyes,

[36] "A New Battle of Karbala," *The Graphics of Revolution and War*, published 15 October 2018, https://www.lib.uchicago.edu/collex/exhibits/graphics-revolution-and-war-iranian-poster-arts/new-battle-karbala/.

posing like the Pietà, her large Dalí-esque hands cradling an armful of red tulips as an icon of martyrdom. The melting red of blood with the yellow of the desert foregrounds the orange scenery. In Chalipa's art, the individual woman serves as the representative of the collective consciousness. War becomes a sacred and aesthetic zone. These paintings can be hung on the wall for adornment, and they need not be covered. There is no shame, disgust, or shock in the war they depict. They encourage the viewer to praise the beauty of stoic heroism.

Figure 1.2 *Sacrifice*. Kazem Chalipa, 1981.[37]

Oil on canvas, 78.75" x 118".
Courtesy of the artist Kazem Chalipa.

Naser Palangi, a prominent artist of the revolution and the Iran-Iraq War, offers a contrasting portrayal of women in his artwork. While Chalipa focuses on women's sacrificial offering and inward-facing mourning, Palangi depicts the female combatants of southern Iran as inheritors of Zeinab's legacy. These women courageously take up arms to fight against the occupation forces. In three paintings created in 1980, Palangi captures his observations of the intense

---

[37] *Sacrifice* (Kazem Chalipa, 1981) - ایثار

fighting that occurred in southern Iran when Iraqi forces crossed the borders and occupied Iranian cities. Each painting presents only the upper bodies of the women, with their prominent feature being the rifles they hold with Dali-esque hands, symbolizing their extraordinary power. Although their gazes are averted from the audience, their expressions are stern and determined. One painting, entitled *A Woman Holding a Rifle*[38], depicts a woman with her gaze directed forward, while signs of destruction blend into the gray-toned background, barely sketched with quick strokes. The contours of her head and hand are clearly discernible. In the other two paintings, the women's bodies dissolve into the background, leaving only their large hands, rifles, and unwavering faces in the foreground. Their relentless and uncompromising gazes are directed upward while a devastated landscape dissolves within their immense eyes and hands.

Figure 1.3 *Resistance*. Kazem Chalipa, 1983.[39]

Oil on canvas, 47.25" x 39.4".
Courtesy of the artist Kazem Chalipa.

   This depiction of Iranian women in wartime, despite its superficial appearance of empowerment, is questionable. In his essay, "Regarding the Pain of Women: Questions of Gender and the Arts of Holocaust Memory," James Young raises an intriguing question: are we truly witnessing the anguish experienced by women, or are we merely projecting our own interpretations onto them, viewing them as

---

[38] *A Woman Holding a Rifle* (Naser Palangi, ca. 1980s) - زنی با اسلحه

[39] *Resistance* (Kazem Chalipa, 1983) - مقاومت

symbols of resistance, innocence, and renewal? Young highlights the historical context of the Holocaust and the limited narratives surrounding the suffering endured by both men and women during Nazi rule. While stories of hunger, separation, and deportation were shared, there was a notable absence of accounts addressing "sexual exploitation, religious modesty, rape, childbirth, or abortions."[40] These aspects of women's experiences were frequently omitted from conventional Holocaust narratives. Young contends that the tales of women's vulnerability and physical torment are often overshadowed by their portrayal as symbols of resistance. Female suffering during the Iran-Iraq War has similarly been hidden by ideological efforts. The artists of the Revolution and Sacred Defense, by projecting their own perspectives, tend to depict women according to desired stereotypes that align with values associated with the domestic sphere and a conservative patriarchal society.

Figure 1.4 *Desert* Kazem Chalipa, 1984.[41]

Oil on canvas, 63" x 51".
Courtesy of the artist Kazem Chalipa.

---

[40] James E. Young, *The Stages of Memory: Reflections on Memorial Art, Loss, and the Spaces Between* (Amherst: University of Massachusetts Press, 2016), 110.

[41] *Desert* (Kazem Chalipa, 1984) - بیابان

Unlike the art of the Sacred Defense, Goya's etching Plate 7 from *The Disasters of War*[42] series, titled "What Courage!" (Figure 1.5), stands in stark opposition to the fixation on collective identity in women that disregards their individual suffering. The scene depicted is based on a real event; a woman named Augustina Zaragoza is said to have defended the city when she realized that the Spanish militia had been killed or were too injured to fight. In contrast to Palangi's mural, where women are depicted as serene and honorable, Goya's artwork presents a fearless female figure firing an iron cannon and using a pile of bodies to create a grotesque staircase. The portrayal of women in Palangi's work highlights their wartime demeanor as composed and dignified, distinct from the intense and aggressive scene depicted by Goya. Two additional plates, 13 and 30, portray the profound humiliation endured by women through scenes of rape. In this series of plates, the brutality of war reaches its most horrific form. These images depict the violation of women who represent not only individuals but also mothers, sisters, the very essence of a nation and its people, and the core of humanity itself. War not only dismantles and degrades the physical body but also inflicts lasting changes upon one's sense of self.

Figure 1.5 "What Courage!" Francisco Goya, Plate 7 of *The Disasters of War*, 1810.

Etching, 6" x 8.18". The Metropolitan Museum of Art.
Source: CC0. https://www.metmuseum.org/art/collection/search/380642

Plate 14 of *The Disasters of War*, titled "The Way Is Hard!" (Figure 1.6), showcases Goya's disillusionment with the promises of the Enlightenment and the hypocritical preaching of the Church. The title itself is derived from a biblical passage, "For the gate is narrow and the way is hard that leads to life, and those

---

[42] In the original Spanish: *Los Desastres de la Guerra*

who find it are few" (Matthew 7:14), yet Goya's drawing completely mocks this notion. In the center, a ladder is positioned between two poles, forming a supposed doorway or gateway. Surrounding this doorway are lifeless or dying bodies, with additional deceased men hanging beyond the passage, seemingly bound to the same poles. Three men exert their efforts to push and pull another immobilized man up the ladder. Adjacent to the ladder stands a priest, wearing a smug expression on his face as he points upward with one hand. Amidst exhaustion and disbelief, one of the suffering men gazes in the direction indicated by the priest. Goya purposefully frames the top section of the illustration closely to the blood-soaked scene on Earth, leaving the viewer questioning whether this gateway leads anywhere substantial – the heavens are not present in even a literal sense. This reading is supported by art historian Richard Muther's interpretation of many of Goya's engravings:

> Goya preached Nihilism in the home of belief, he denied everything, believed nothing, doubted of everything, even of that peace and liberty that he hoped to be at hand. That old Spanish art of religion and dogma was changed under his hands to an art of negation and sarcasm.[43]

Figure 1.6 "The Way is Hard!" Francisco Goya, Plate 14 of *The Disasters of War*, ca. 1810.

Etching, 5.6" x 6.6". The Metropolitan Museum of Art.
Source: CC0. https://www.metmu seum.org/ art/collection/search/333976

Goya does not suggest to the viewer that the world is inherently a safe place: "The world is a masquerade," he says. "Face, dress, and voice, all are false. All wish

---

[43] Richard Muther, *The History of Modern Painting* (New York: Henry Holt and Co., 1895), 66.

to appear what they are not, all deceive, and nobody knows anybody. "[44] Goya posits that a genuine understanding of the true nature of war, in light of human suffering, can only be achieved through a deliberate negation of ideology, politics, and religion. By stripping away these constructs, one can peer beyond the veils of biased perspectives and confront the stark realities of war. Goya's perspective challenges the optimistic ideals propagated during the Enlightenment, revealing their inadequacy and naivety in the face of the harsh and brutal consequences of armed conflict as Plate 69, "Nada," suggests, as a skeleton rises from his grave to inscribe a single word: "Nothing. "[45]

The perspective of Iranian revolutionaries differed significantly from that of Goya, despite the parallel between his art depicting resistance against Napoleon's invasion and the war and resistance against Iraqies experienced in Iran. Prior to and in the early years following the 1979 Revolution, Iranian subjects were portrayed as individuals fed up with the social, economic, and political conditions under the Pahlavī dynasty. Their depictions screamed in agony with wide-open eyes and mouths, resembling skeletal figures enduring a difficult and infuriating demise.[46] Following the triumph of the revolution, however, Iranian art asserted that a remarkable transformation had occurred within these once agitated and screaming individuals. They became humble and spiritually inclined subjects, prepared to make ultimate sacrifices in defense of their now idealized homeland. A homeland that had achieved such an elevated state of perfection after the Revolution that objections were nonexistent and dissent was conspicuously absent, reflecting a meticulously constructed hegemonic harmony.

Hussein Khosrowjerdi, an iconic figure within the circle of artists since the early stages of the Islamic Revolution, created *Cry*[47] in 1980, drawing inspiration from Edvard Munch's *The Scream* (1893). The screaming subjects, portrayed as alien-like and unrecognizable as humans, are depicted in a state of agitation, tearing their clothes and bellowing with gaping mouths and furious eyes, piercing the viewer's expectations. The blending of colors enhances the intensity of their protest and opposition against the pre-revolution authorities. However, after the Revolution's victory and during the Iran-Iraq

---

[44] Pierre Gassier et al, *The Life and Complete Works of Francisco Goya* (New York: Reynal and Morrow, 1971), 131.

[45] The original title says, "Nothing! That's what it says." The academy in Spain later decided that this was a very atheistic pessimism, and they softened the title to say "The Event Will Tell" (Gassier et al., *The Life and Complete Works*, 220).

[46] See for example Siroos Moghaddam's *Tyranny* (1978), *From Birth to Death* (1978) and many of Nosratollah Moslemian's paintings such as *Immigration* (1975), *Shadow in Blood* (1977) and *Strike of Oil Workers* (1978).

[47] *Cry* (Hussein Khosrowjerdi, 1980) - فریاد

War, Khosrowjerdi shifted his representation of Iranian fighters to dignified revolutionary preachers of resistance and sacrifice. In *Light of History*[48] (1984, Figure 1.8), an archetypal martyr figure gazes toward the sky, kneeling before his imminent demise. A radiant light emanates from the tip of his weapon, symbolizing the redemptive and enlightening nature of his death in war. The iconic colors of green and red infuse the scene with historical and religious significance. The green headband, reminiscent of the martyrs of Karbala in the 7th century, intertwines with the red of the soldier's blood, alluding to the bloodshed of Imam Hossein and his companions. Additionally, the green band encircles the earth, personifying and making it a sympathetic witness to the soldier's sacrificial, heroic death. In this context, death in war is equated with spiritual ecstasy and redemption.

In the midst of the feverish atmosphere of war, it is often observed that the body becomes a political symbol, embodying notions of courage, heroism, and an otherworldly presence while simultaneously demonizing the unseen and excluded enemy. War sociologist Kevin McSorley aptly describes war as more than just politics; it is a lived experience etched into the bodies and minds of men and women. War occupies countless bodies in diverse ways, profoundly shaping lives and redefining what it means to be human.[49] In Khosrowjerdi's painting, there is a notable absence of pain and suffering in the face of the dying soldier. His eyes are closed, and as he succumbs to death, his face is turned away from the viewer; just like the averted faces depicted in Chalipa's works, the soldier is portrayed as detached from the viewer's material world. This representation imposes a specific meaning on death and enforces a narrow interpretation of traumatic history. In stark contrast, Otto Dix's "Dying Soldier" [50] (1924) presents a visceral portrayal of Western/European victims of violence, bluntly depicting the facial contortions of pain in war violence. Their deaths differ from those who resist an imposed war; the death of a resistance fighter fighting against imperialism assumes meanings that extend beyond mere destruction and decomposition.

These artistic portrayals highlight not only the complexities of war but also the divergent narratives surrounding its purpose. The Iranian soldier's symbolic death in *Light of History* serves a particular cause, while the Western victims of violence in Dix's artwork present a perspective of meaninglessness. The death of a resistance fighter carries a significance that transcends surface-level

---

[48] *Light of History* (Hussein Khosrowjerdi, 1984) - شمع تاریخ
[49] Kevin McSorley, *War and the Body: Militarisation, Practice and Experience* (New York: Routledge, 2013), 1.
[50] In the original German: "Sterbender Soldat"

destruction, shedding light on the multifaceted nature of war experiences and the varying interpretations of its consequences.

The reduction of individual suffering to a singular dimension of martyrdom, as observed in *Light of History* and the other works discussed here, highlights the precarious transformation of anti-imperialism into an unquestioning nationalism, underscoring the potential dangers inherent in such a shift. Fanon had himself predicted that the conception of a "national literature" and "national culture" might develop into xenophobia and intolerance; for Fanon, national culture held limited potential.[51] Just as it could help define a native culture against the crushing assault of the colonizer, it could also return a country to its pre-colonial past through the adoption of a pre-colonial culture that would not guarantee any benefit to the working classes and the oppressed. Although he was an advocate for a national culture, Fanon believed that its effectiveness relied on the national culture's accounting for the economic conditions of the working classes. He incisively noted that culture is not stable, must be dynamic and open to change, and must be critically evaluated so as to bring in appropriate changes rather than stay fixed in its older forms. For Fanon, there is a parallel between the old colonial masters and the elite of postcolonial nations, wherein the elites inhabit the positions of power once occupied by their white masters, while the corruption and oppression of the working classes persist at the hands of fellow natives.[52] Since the 1970s, post-war cultural and artistic production in Iran has remained fixated on a religious revolutionary vision and a hegemonic national literature and culture that insures a collective identity while neglecting the needs of the working class and victims of war who continue to remain unintegrated into the means of social, political, and cultural production. The voice of the victim is the voice of weakness, and weakness challenges the status quo.

Aligned with the prevailing sentiment, artists like Morteza Goodarzi Dibaj lamented through the published collection of artwork, *Committed Social and Religious Art in Iran: Paintings of Revolution* (2009), yearning for a resurgence of revolutionary and religious fervor within contemporary visual art. Goodarzi's desire was to return to an era where piety and spiritually significant events were depicted, creating art that resonated with the revolutionary spirit.[53] However, it is important to acknowledge the inherently problematic nature of Goodarzi's statement. While Goodarzi advocates for a revival of past ideals, he overlooks the need for Iranian society to articulate the post-war crisis it currently faces.

---

[51] Fanon, *The Wretched of the Earth*, 206-248.

[52] K. Pramod Nayar, *Contemporary Literature and Cultural Theory: From Structuralism to Ecocriticism* (London: Pearson Education India, 2009), 158-159.

[53] Morteza Goodarzi Dibaj, *Committed Social and Religious Art in Iran: Paintings of Revolution* (Tehran: Farhangestan e Honor Publications, 2009).

Just as the 1979 Revolution and Iran-Iraq War allowed Iranian society to express its values at that time, the present era demands an opportunity to address the multifaceted challenges and complexities that have emerged in the aftermath. The preservation of religious national identity has (perhaps inadvertently) created a void, effectively silencing the voices of those who survived the war but continue to endure suffering as a result of its violence. These individuals strive to break free from the confines of conservative conformity and demand that their trauma and suffering be acknowledged in their full material reality.

Traumatic Realism and a Link Between Cultures: Art of Resistance in a Globalized World

Rothberg highlights three essential requirements for understanding and representing the Holocaust: the need for documentation, the exploration of the boundaries of representation, and the courageous dissemination of discussions about the events from a social standpoint rather than a spiritual or transcendental perspective.[54] These demands emphasize the importance of capturing and preserving historical evidence, critically examining the limitations of representing such a massively traumatic event and engaging in open and risky public discourse. By adopting Rothberg's framework for understanding and representing historical trauma in the context of the Holocaust, we can apply similar principles to our examination of the Art of Resistance in the Iran-Iraq case. This approach allows us to explore "the intersections of the psychic and the social, the discursive and the material, and the extreme and every day" while recognizing the demands for documentation, reflection on the limits of representation, and "the risky public circulation of discourses on these events."[55] By considering realism, modernism (and symbolism as a subgenre within the modernist movement), and postmodernism as persistent responses to the demands of history, we can gain a deeper understanding of the socio-aesthetic dimensions of art's ability to address and represent traumatic experiences in a globalized world.

Traumatic realism, as discussed by Rothberg, beyond being a genre of representation, "provides an aesthetic and cognitive solution to the conflicting demands"[56] in representation and understanding of traumatic historical events. Established modes of understanding advocate for an impossible mode of understanding by linking factual destruction and mutilation with the spiritual, transcendental, and immaterial concepts of redemption, regeneration, and sacrificial martyrdom. However, the post-war world, the generations born after

---

[54] Rothberg, *Traumatic Realism*, 7.
[55] Rothberg, *Traumatic Realism*, 7.
[56] Rothberg, *Traumatic Realism*, 9.

the events, and those victims suffering the material consequences of the war need a mediated approach that can address the historical facts with its material consequences and yet the immaterial and unrepresentable experience of pain. The unspeakable and immaterial in this sense, as deconstructive as it may appear, does not allude to immaterial theology or teleological closure; rather, it circles back to the material limitations and limits of linguistic capabilities of representing the traumatic and the painfully real. While those who fight in support of the purported cause of wars have historically been remembered in only one specific way, the literary and artistic representations of war specifically written and produced by those who have experienced its traumatic violence typically depict a reality that is not quite so black and white.

John Halaka, an artist of Palestinian descent, has embraced the traumatic realist form in his series of works that act as an ethical and moral response to human suffering, as a form of resistance to the complete erasure of a nation. He views his approach to the arts as the only solution for ending violence and preserving the memories of the genocide of the Palestinians. Halaka imaginatively, tirelessly, and optimistically dreams of initiating "a dialogue with the viewer that could hopefully instigate transformation, one person at a time."[57] He presents the trauma of displacement, occupation, and the culture of resistance not by advocating for a revolutionary armed struggle against the perpetrator, displaying the heroic martyrdom of the freedom fighter, or even by illustrating the destroyed cultural icons and symbols of Palestinian nationality, like other artists of resistance such as Ismail Shammout and Silman Mansour.[58] Rather, it is his belief in the universality of compassion, empathy, and respect for the dignity of all human beings that informs his artwork. As an example, his earlier series of artwork titled *Remember to Forget* (1993-1995) serves as a contemplation on the sociological aspect of martyrdom, portraying martyrs who are depicted as disfigured and devoid of cultural symbols. This contradicts the conventional portrayal of martyrs as spiritually uplifting figures. He asserts that he wants "to raise questions in the viewer's mind about his/her psychological and political relationship to the images of martyrs glorified in public monuments" and to reflect on "the benign acceptance of a mythology of martyrdom, created through the institutional promotion of personal sacrifice and collective suffering."[59] Halaka addresses the occupation and resistance of Palestine by highlighting in brush and ink the unspeakable emotional and psychological pain of ordinary human beings who have been victims of the traumas of expulsion and cultural

[57] John Halaka, "Artist Statement," John Halaka, http://johnhalaka.com/artiststatements.html.
[58] For a comprehensive and in-depth study and analysis of Palestinian art, from its roots in folk art and traditional Christian and Islamic painting to the nationalistic themes and diverse media used today, see Ankori, Gannit. *Palestinian Art*. London: Reaktion, 2006.
[59] Halaka, "Artist Statement."

extermination. For him, war, occupation, and displacement are not mere political battles involving "good" and "evil," in which the only "good" people are those who are celebrated in the media for their heroic deaths on the battlefield. For Halaka, every individual scream of pain and cry of suffering that comes as a consequence of war should be remembered.

In his recent series of drawings titled *Ghosts of Presence/Bodies of Absence*, Halaka combines personal images and narratives of Palestinian refugees with the ghostly, haunting, and perpetual presence of traumatic, repressed memories resulting from a denied and destroyed homeland, as seen in the piece "Desire " (Figure 1.7).[60] Through the fusion of portraits of Palestinian refugees with images of demolished Palestinian villages, Halaka creates a compelling depiction that exposes the psychological and physical devastation resulting from the continuous erasure of Palestinian history and culture by colonial forces. Through his artwork, Halaka delves into the enduring struggle of survivors to navigate and bear witness to the ongoing tragedies experienced by multiple generations of Palestinians; their struggle to be heard becomes visualized in the dismantled bodies featured throughout his series *Remember to Forget* (particularly in "If Headless Figures Could Talk, Would They Speak of Their Sacrifice," seen in Figure 1.8). The themes of displacement and loss of home through violent expulsion, the resilient pursuit for return, and the active remembrance of a shattered homeland and culture are all central concerns for Palestinian survivors and, consequently, for the artist himself. The exploration of traumatic memory and the quest for belonging resonate as recurring motifs in Halaka' s work. These motifs serve as powerful tools for cultural preservation and personal resistance. Halaka' s artwork boldly suggests that survival and resistance are interconnected endeavors that actively challenge the erasure of Indigenous peoples, both physically and culturally, imposed by colonial powers.

Recurrence, repetition, and reliving the past are at the heart of the traumatic experience and, thus, the primary symptoms of post-traumatic culture. A traumatic encounter is defined as an experience that is too unexpected to be fully known and assimilated at the time it occurs but that imposes itself later on repeatedly in the nightmares, flashbacks, and actions of survivors; a haunting return that demands understanding and witness.[61] In many of the drawings of the *Ghosts of Presence/Bodies of Absence* collection, images of place are constructed out of the repetition of a single, rubber-stamped word like "survivors," "forgotten," "resistance," "return," "freedom," "desire" and "memory." Violence has a profound

---

[60] The narrative portraits of refugees can be seen in Halaka's recent body of work, titled *Portraits of Denial and Desire*, created between 2012-2016; while images of destroyed and denied Palestinian landscape can be seen in his series *Landscape of Desire*, created between 2009-2013.

[61] Caruth, *Unclaimed Experience*, 4.

impact on individuals, creating a deep psychological space within them that can be likened to a crypt – a burial place for something cherished and deeply connected to their identity. This crypt is formed as a result of the traumatic experience, serving as a repository for the secrets and silences that accompany it. Within this crypt, the individual grapples with the hidden and unspoken aspects of their suffering, often struggling to find a means of expression.

Figure 1.7 "Desire," John Halaka, #18, *Ghosts of Presence/Bodies of Absence*, 2016.

Ink and rubber stamp on printed drawing paper, 6" x 8.6".
Courtesy of the artist, John Halaka. www.JohnHalaka.com

Figure 1.8 "If Headless Figures Could Talk #3" John Halaka, *Remember to Forget*, 1993.

Ink on paper, 15" x 10".
Courtesy of the artist, John Halaka. www.JohnHalaka

Cryptonyms (words or symbols with hidden or disguised meanings) can act as a pathway to this crypt, offering a way for individuals to confront and engage with their traumatic experiences. These cryptonyms serve as linguistic tools that enable individuals to navigate the depths of their psychic crypt, attempting to exorcize the lingering effects of the traumatic events they have endured. By employing cryptonyms, individuals can bring these hidden experiences into the realm of social discourse, seeking to establish a connection between their personal struggles and the larger social context.[62] In Halaka's innovative representation of traumatic memory, the viewer is confronted by the obsessive, sometimes involuntary remembrance of the destruction of place, loss, longing for return, and a stubborn persistence in bearing witness to some ignored and forgotten wound that nevertheless is still active and open for many Palestinians. For Palestinians, as Halaka states, "memory is the engine of their return. Memory allows the Palestinians to envision and to seek the denied security of their homeland; it enables them to creatively design the re-construction of their shattered society."[63]

In each and every image of destruction and ruin in Halaka's drawings, blended into the rubble, is a shadowy reflection of a face or a pair of eyes of a real victim. The combination of this human reality hovering over the fading, gradually warped memory of destruction allows for a dual interpretation of the image. In every destroyed home, there are eternal ghosts of lost human souls. Their constant, subconscious presence counterbalances the political absence created by the barbaric and ongoing destruction of an entire people's history. The psychological, political, and physical experiences of presence and absence that are forever engraved in the memories of Palestinian survivors pervade Halaka's drawings. The faded imagery of traumatic history layered in Halaka's drawings dissolves the representational character of the images almost to the point of abstraction. In contrast, the obsessive repetition of single words that shape the imagery confirms the fact that what cannot be articulately communicated registers in memory as an image. This artistic representation of trauma in *Ghosts of Presence/Bodies of Absence* suggests that despite the constant attempt at the ethnic and cultural cleansing of the Palestinian people and the consequent denial and oppression of their tragedies, the traumatic memories of destruction and oppression are not destructible; in fact, they persistently repeat themselves in resistance to their erasure.

The success of Halaka's vision in this series is rooted in his proximity to the crypt of the refugees' psychological existence. Through the shape of holes, gaps,

---

[62] Gabriele Schwab, "Writing Against Memory and Forgetting," *Literature and Medicine* 25, no. 1 (2006): 95-121.
[63] Halaka, "Artist Statement."

openings, windows, and doors in the midst of rubble, Halaka creates a pathway to the abyss of traumatic memories. The construction of these gaps and openings in the drawings exemplifies both the impossibility of adequately representing the traumatic experience and the resistance of the traumatized psyche to closure without being attached or alluding to a solid and recognizable structure. His artwork displays the shapeless and phantom nature of pain and suffering alongside the desire and hope for justice and freedom. Halaka's artistic endeavor aims to address universal aspects of humanity by removing specific cultural identities from his artworks. This deliberate absence of defining characteristics serves to emphasize the shared experiences of displacement and tragedy among marginalized groups, particularly the Palestinians and others who have endured persecution. By stripping away cultural markers, Halaka highlights the parallel tragedies of displacement, drawing attention to the interconnected nature of suffering. This artistic choice reflects a moral perspective that emphasizes the common humanity of individuals affected by violence. Through his work, Halaka seeks to establish a dialogue between the wounded body and psyche and the broader world, enabling the witnessing of other histories of violence and cultivating empathy towards marginalized and affected communities.

While the art of the revolution in the Islamic Republic often emphasizes religious and ideological themes as tools of resistance, portraying an idealized vision of the revolution, war, and its leaders, Halaka's art takes a different approach. Halaka's approach challenges nationalist, colonial, and imperial politics of division that perpetuate reciprocal exclusivity, separating and isolating different zones and peoples. By refusing to emphasize cultural divisions, his art supports the idea that resistance to such politics necessitates transcending separation and isolation. Instead, it promotes recognizing shared experiences of suffering, fostering connections, and working towards a more inclusive and empathetic understanding of humanity.

The Enigma of Survival and the Search for Meaning: When the Victims Ask Questions

In Caruth's understanding of a trauma narrative, she suggests that at its core lies a duality – a "double telling" – that oscillates between two interrelated crises. The first crisis pertains to the experience of death or the traumatic event itself, capturing the overwhelming and unbearable nature of the initial impact. The second crisis involves the aftermath of the event, specifically the struggle to cope with survival and continued existence in the wake of such a traumatic experience. To Lifton, the imprint of death becomes a central aspect of the survivor's experience, influencing their perception, thoughts, and emotions. While the crisis of death highlights the unbearable nature of the traumatic event itself, the crisis of life pertains to the ongoing challenges and struggles that come with surviving and carrying the weight of the traumatic experience.

Expanding on the comprehension of trauma narratives and the interconnected crises of death and life, certain visual artists have demonstrated a keen interest in unraveling the enigma of survival, challenging the dominant ideological structures of hegemonic politics. Mohsen Makhmalbaf's film *Marriage of the Blessed* [64] (1989) stands as one of the most audacious visual representations to date of the post-traumatic experience of the Iran-Iraq War, delving deeply into the shattered psyche of a soldier. As one of the pioneering cinematic endeavors to critically examine the individual and societal impacts of revolution and war, this film masterfully captures the debilitating effects of post-traumatic stress disorder. Makhmalbaf, once a radical revolutionary opposing Mohammad Rezā Shāh Pahlavī's regime, here fearlessly brings to light and immortalizes the suffering of the marginalized characters in his work. In direct contrast to the Islamic Republic's inclination to suppress non-conformist and visceral portrayals of the physical and psychological realities of suffering, Makhmalbaf vividly depicts the disintegration, decomposition, and what Elaine Scarry describes as the "unmaking" of a soldier within the context of the Iran-Iraq War. Haji, a photojournalist, becomes the central protagonist of this influential film, confined to a hospital for shell shock after his harrowing experiences in the war. *Marriage of the Blessed* traces Haji's journey of constant medicalization, pathologizing, and his arduous process of reintegrating into society following his release. Through compelling filmic techniques such as striking montages of black and white shots, dramatic flash-bulb lighting, and intrusive close-ups, Makhmalbaf skillfully portrays how bodies are manipulated, transformed, and recycled to serve the ideological objectives of the state.

The narrative commences with a powerful long traveling shot, guiding the audience through hospital hallways and culminating in a mental ward, where Haji and fellow veterans grapple with various forms of mania. Utilizing still photographs, film excerpts, graffiti, and billboard art, Makhmalbaf establishes a poignant visual framework, immersing viewers in the complex realities of post-war trauma and its profound impact on individuals and society. The camera follows a hospital tray on a swiftly moving cart through dim hallways, focusing on the array of medical instruments. The cart eventually enters a room filled with veterans who move about in a disoriented manner, resembling individuals in a state of lunacy. The veterans' self-addressed monologues during the theatrical re-enactments of their battlefield experiences are particularly noteworthy. Through the use of specific language, such as the cry of "Holy martyrs!" during a flashback to a battlefield explosion and the plea that, "we are

---

[64] *Marriage of the Blessed* (Mohsen Makhmalbaf, 1989) - عروسی خوبان

in a critical situation, send angels," accompanied by a tin pot on one veteran's head, the film juxtaposes the concept of war's sanctity with the portrayal of male protagonists imprisoned within a mental hospital. Regardless of whether their suffering is ideological, physical, or psychological, these protagonists find themselves confined in this institutional setting.

As a physician begins to draw blood from Haji's hand, his traumatic memories of the battlefield resurface and manifest in a visual flashback. In one poignant moment, Haji falls from the shock of an explosion and instinctively reaches out to embrace a hand touching his face. The subsequent reframing of the shot reveals that the hand has been severed from its body, and another reframing exposes blood flowing from another soldier's shoulder. This powerful imagery captures an image, an indelible imprint of the event, etched in the survivor's memory, which is then transmitted and communicated to the viewer. The flashback to this extreme moment unveils the protagonist's persistent and disturbing intrusion, as well as his heightened vigilance in response to even the most innocuous sounds and sights. The constant reliving of the traumatic experience in the present becomes an integral part of his existence.

Drawing from a verse in the Quran – "الَّذِينَ إِذَا أَصَابَتْهُمْ مُصِيبَةٌ قَالُوا إِنَّا لِلَّهِ وَإِنَّا إِلَيْهِ رَاجِعُونَ" [65] – the Islamic State of Iran preaches a religious perspective that regards the earthly realm as transient and fleeting, considering it to be the lowest form of existence. It contrasts the temporary nature of earthly life with the magnificence and everlasting nature of the afterlife. According to this belief, martyrdom in the service of God is viewed as the pinnacle of human perfection.[66] The physical and material reality of life and the human body are, in this belief system, replaced by the promise of paradise, where participation in war is idealized as a religious form of "jihad," a gate to eternal happiness. Makhmalbaf subverts this ideology, foregrounding the very materiality of suffering by those who survive and continue their complicated lives after the war. The misfortunes are often tragic, and the hellish psychiatric facility is far from perfect. It is in the deconstruction of both the material and immaterial world of the survivor that Makhmalbaf seeks to represent the post-traumatic condition of those who survive to live the historical trauma. As Elaine Scarry argues,

> …the incontestable reality of the body – the body in pain, the body maimed, the body dead and hard to dispose of – is separated from its source and conferred on an ideology or issue or instance of political authority… The winning issue or ideology achieves for a time the force

[65] In English: "who when misfortune falls upon them say: surely we are Allah's and to him do we return."
[66] Jolyon P. Mitchell, *Promoting Peace, Inciting Violence: The Role of Religion and Media* (New York: Routledge, 2012), 59.

and status of material "fact" by the sheer material weight of the multitudes of damaged and opened human bodies.[67]

The stability of any political state, a very material reality, is founded on the material base of the human body. However, the wound, the crisis of suffering itself, becomes a symbol of non-material abstraction. Julia Kristeva similarly emphasizes the significance of the body, proposing that it is through the body that transcendence is possible, understanding transcendence "as a horizon of possibility for futurity, not as a flight into a metaphysical and disembodied beyond." The subjects of Sacred Defense art – the body and its drives – are thus faced with a crisis of non-representation.[68] In direct contrast, *Marriage of the Blessed* depicts the significance of the body, within which the psychological and physical consequences of war are entangled and become highly political. Black and white shots of poverty and crime in dark corners of the city through the lens of the shell-shocked journalist Haji resembles Goya and Dix's stylistic innovations of depicting brutal realities. The aestheticization in the symbolic form of the wounded subject's post-war condition takes advantage of the reality of the suffering subject.

In the film's central climax, Haji photographs the guests in attendance at his wedding. The contrast between what he sees through the lens of his camera, as opposed to what he sees in real life, underscores the contradiction between the idealized promises of the redistribution of wealth according to revolutionary rhetoric and the material realities of the new wealthy class. A subsequent shot fixes Haji's gaze on two of his comrades. He sees their young, glowing, cheerful, and vigorous faces before the war through the camera and then their disfigured, broken bodies after the war. Flashbacks of vibrant pre-war imagery quickly shift with the sound of the shutter to a black-and-white post-war traumatized reality. In this shot, his gaze on the young veterans is contemplative and full of bewilderment and agony. His empathy is so complete that he must be physically removed to avert his eyes from the disfigured and transformed veterans.

Just as Fanon gradually shifted away from a purely socio-cultural view of national identity – instead suggesting a more materialist-economic, dynamic approach – for post-revolution and post-war artists like Makhmalbaf, the economic degradation of society after the War became a site for communicating the message of traumatic survival. For Makhmalbaf, it is only through the realization of the material reality of the body and its suffering, only through the juxtaposition of the extreme and the everyday in the life of a survivor, that the complexity of

---

[67] Elaine Scarry, *The Body in Pain: The Making and Unmaking of the World* (New York: Oxford University Press, 1985), 62.

[68] Fanny Söderbäck, "Revolutionary Time: Revolt as Temporal Return," *Signs* 37, no. 2 (2012): 320.

traumatic experience can be delivered. Rothberg argues that traumatic realism focuses on the historical "event" without employing explicit and detailed mimetic representation. However, it aims to engage and challenge its audience, compelling them to confront their connection to post-traumatic culture and undergo a transformative experience.[69]

By focusing on the historical "event," these works, such as Makhmalbaf's film, shed light on the enduring effects of trauma without relying solely on descriptive details. The intention is not to provide a straightforward representation of the event itself but rather to provoke a response in the audience that prompts them to acknowledge their relationship to the culture shaped by trauma. Through this transformative engagement, the audience is encouraged to examine their role in post-traumatic culture and consider the implications of collective trauma on personal and societal levels. In essence, traumatic realism challenges the audience to confront the lingering effects of trauma and to reflect on their position within the larger framework of a post-traumatic world. For Makhmalbaf, the religiously abstracted, fictionalized structure and representation of the Iran-Iraq War do not accurately reflect the harsh mental and physical transformation of the soldiers in peacetime and the postwar structure of society. For this reason, when Haji ultimately breaks free from the hospital, he wanders the streets of Tehran to become the subject of a different artist's lens, in this case, of the photographer's gaze.

In contrast to postcolonial theory's critique of the Western notion of individuality and the psychological interpretation of trauma, contemporary postcolonial and anti-imperial artists have increasingly focused on the significance of the body and personal experiences of pain and suffering. This shift does not seek to erase the history of imperial and colonial influence on traumatic cultures, nor does it blindly adopt Western ideas of trauma. It also does not aim to oversimplify the societal, political, and cultural complexities as a singular entity. Instead, the intention is to create a dialogue between the individual and collective voices, recognizing the importance of individual pain and suffering without sacrificing their singularity and understanding history in the present circumstances, an approach to traumatic events for which Rothberg is advocating. Rothberg associates the concept of the unknowable nature of the Holocaust with the postmodern perspective, which emphasizes the contextualization of historical events within their present representation. In other words, instead of viewing the Holocaust from an objective standpoint that assumes a timeless truth, the postmodern approach recognizes the influence of the present circumstances on our understanding and interpretation of the event. The desacralization of the Holocaust refers to the stripping away of its sacred or untouchable status,

---

[69] Rothberg, *Traumatic Realism*, 103.

allowing for a more critical examination of its representation in light of contemporary perspectives and discourses.

Prolific film director Ebrahim Hatamikia has also turned a critical gaze on the post-traumatic consequences of war for its victims, their positions in postwar society, and their relation to societies that are fast forgetting them. *From Karkheh to Rhein*[70] (1992) is one of Hatamikia's films, which remains the most affectionate, detailed, and revolutionary representation of the postwar and post-traumatic dilemma of veterans of war; it is also Hatamikia's most retrospective examination of his role as a conformist who has spent much of his own life as a soldier.[71] In *From Karkheh to Rhein,* the director challenges conventional notions of the "Sacred Defense " as a unified Iranian narrative of holy war that extends beyond its borders. The movie depicts war veterans who have suffered severe injuries, and tragically, a significant number of them do not survive the life-threatening wounds they incurred in foreign lands, particularly in Germany. The main character, Said, is blinded as a result of his wartime experiences and seeks treatment to restore his vision. However, he is later diagnosed with leukemia due to exposure to chemicals. The plot's international backdrop introduces an element of cultural irony. It prompted a call for cross-cultural discussions with Western and European allies who were directly involved in the victimization of numerous people by supplying arms and chemical weapons to the oppressive Iraqi government.

Hatamikia tackles the issue of imperial technological capabilities that both create weapons of mass destruction and offer remedies for their effects. The film highlights the neglected perspective of the West within the genre of the "Sacred Defense" and juxtaposes it with the experiences of the victims. The idealistic Said engages in conversations with his severely wounded comrade, Kazem, who desires asylum in Germany, holds bitter criticisms of the war, and undergoes an existential crisis, questioning the role of God in the sufferings he endures. The director deviates from the stereotypes of war that typically depict opposing forces, including the East and the West, and challenges the early revolutionary slogans of "No East, No West, only the Islamic Republic." The erasure of geographic boundaries facilitates a mutual dialogue between the East and the West, as well as between perpetrators and victims, bringing forth a nuanced exploration of the complexities of war.

Hatamikia, a dedicated revolutionary, takes a different path from the usual narrative. He shifts his attention to the experiences of soldiers in the aftermath

---

[70] In the original Persian: از کرخه تا راین

[71] For a comprehensive study of the social history of Iranian cinema from the late nineteenth century to the early twenty-first, see Naficy, Hamid. Vol. 1-4 of *A Social History of Iranian Cinema.* Durham: Duke University Press, 2011-2012.

of the war, exploring the difficulties and conflicts they faced in the post-war era. Additionally, he examines their reasons for joining the war and poses inquiries regarding the compromised principles and promises of the revolution that remain unfulfilled. Hatamikia's later films emphasize dialogue and debate among individuals with opposing views and diverse experiences.[72] Unlike Khosrowjerdi's *Light of History*, where the soldier's death is portrayed as didactic, otherworldly, and detached from the human experience, Hatamikia's war veterans, who have become disenchanted with their former convictions, eventually meet the same fate as all human beings on this planet. Regardless of their race, place of origin, or faith, these soldiers experience a slow and agonizing death in a foreign land rather than a dignified martyrdom. In one poignant scene, the wounded Muslim soldier Said retreats in a Christian church, overcome by despair, as he confronts the harsh reality of his damaged and dying body, crumbling like the body of Jesus on the Cross. His relation to his identity and his imminent death is in stark contrast with the romanticized death of a soldier in *Light of History* by Hussein Khosrowjerdi. Said's Crucifixion is surely not without pain. This act of breaking down the boundaries of the East/West dichotomy is a step toward dialogue; he emphasizes the importance of the body in pain without sacrificing the particular history and trauma of this particular war.[73]

"The appearance...of a body, though mutilated," Caruth writes, is "the paradoxical evocation of a referential reality neither fictionalized by direct reference nor formalized into a theoretical abstraction."[74] What Caruth emphasizes here is the unfixed state between a "phenomenal" and "conceptual" world, between "dying" and "living," which "resists being generalized into a conceptual or figural law."[75] Her statements highlight the "double wounding" of trauma survivors, as she refers to it, the difficulty of defining and expressing pain when survivors struggle between an understanding of the event that has befallen them and the suffering of the moment, addressing the paradoxical nature of representing a mutilated body. Caruth argues that the appearance of a mutilated body evokes a reality that cannot be easily categorized as either a direct

---

[72] Shahab Esfandiary, *Iranian Cinema and Globalization: National, Transnational and Islamic Dimensions* (Bristol: Intellect, 2012), 152-162.
[73] While there has been extensive research and scholarly work on post-revolutionary Iranian cinema, only a handful of works has been published on Iranian war cinema or the Cinema of Sacred Defense. See Esfandiary, Shahab. *Iranian Cinema and Globalization: National, Transnational and Islamic Dimensions*. Bristol: Intellect, 2012. See also Khosronejad, Pedram. *Iranian Sacred Defence Cinema: Religion, Martyrdom and National Identity*. Canon Pyon: Sean Kingston Publishing, 2012
[74] Caruth, *Unclaimed Experience*, 92.
[75] Caruth, *Unclaimed Experience*, 93.

representation or a theoretical abstraction. This struggle arises because the reality of trauma resists being neatly encapsulated into predefined conceptual or figural frameworks. The vulnerable body, the body in pain, the body suffering, abolishes assumed differences constructed by social, cultural, political, and geographical boundaries and expresses only a cry for recognition. Survivors bear witness to traumatic events by embodying suffering yet represent it as a singular and individual experience that is hard to theorize and generalize and that resists the imposition of any specific meaning. The vulnerable body in pain rejects all meaning. In the experience of suffering, asserts Harold Schweizer, the "ideology of objectivity, the claims of reason and knowledge, are called into question [...] Philosophical distinctions of body and spirit, sensation and intellect, the universal and particular, the physical and metaphysical, no longer apply. The very law of identity is in crisis."[76] Both Makhmalbaf and Hatamikia's characters face this question of identity in a complex world in which they are no longer the lights of history or the continuation of Shiite revolutionary identity; instead, they are merely dehumanized by pain and swallowed up by the amnesia of a society in which they were once a source of hope and light.

Post-Traumatic Consequences of War in Photography

While the medium of painting in post-war Iran has been central in the state-sponsored symbolic representation of a nationalist, anti-colonial/anti-imperial project, Mehdi Monem's (1951-) realist photography graphically illustrates the individual physical and psychological experience of being blown into fragments and yet survive, only to live a life in pain.[77] Monem's photographs are representative of what it means to lose and how to live with the consequences of this loss in an apolitical environment that propagates the notion of gain and redemption in the hereafter. His images are devoid of any metaphysical, religious, or spiritual meaning. Prosthetic hands and legs, oxygen tanks, blinded eyes, and amputated hands and legs are the objects of his photography. Like Otto Dix, for Monem, too, the reality of traumatic life becomes communicable only through the objects and shapes of dismembered and disfigured bodies. His photographs resist any romantic idealism about survival, asserting instead that "war wounds grow old, but they do not heal." He suggests that "in time, the wounded learn to endure the memory and live with their pain. But the injustice of war does not

---

[76] Harold Schweizer, *Suffering and the Remedy of Art* (Albany: State University of New York Press, 1997), 2.

[77] War photography has been the dominant form of documentation and representation of war in Iran, mostly sponsored by ideological and political agenda of the state. For more on war photography see Saramifar, Younes. "Framing the War in the Post War Era: Exploring the Counter-Narratives in Frames of an Iranian War Photographer Thirty Years After the Ceasefire with Iraq." *Media, War & Conflict* 12, no. 4 (Dec. 2019): 392-410.

end there. War banishes its victims to oblivion only to catch its breath. It can then move on unheeded to reduce other peoples and communities to cinders. "[78] Monem uses his photography to resist such oblivion and forgetfulness, "to register and remind, to break the silence that feeds war," and to close the "road to our purposeful neglect."[79] He views the consequences of war as incurable, as creating both a perpetual traumatic memory and physical reality. He does this not only through depicting the first generation's direct experience of the war but also the second generation's connection to the trauma of their parents that now belongs to them.

Figure 1.9 *Untitled* [taken in Baneh], Mehdi Monem, 2001, photograph. *War Victims*, 2009.

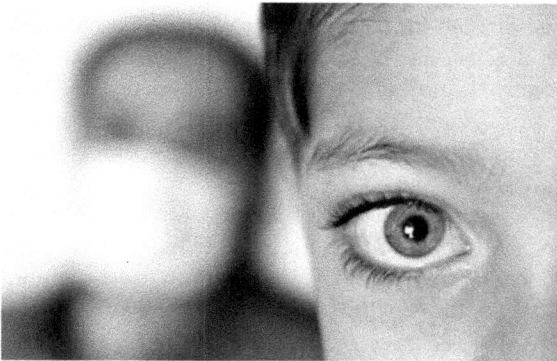

Courtesy of the artist, Mehdi Monem.

In the section titled "Civilian Victims of Chemical Weapons" in his photo book, *War Victims* (2009), a striking image (Figure 1.9) captures the reader's attention – the intense, close-up gaze of a young boy. The composition centers on his right eye, which directly meets the camera and the viewers' eyes.[80] Simultaneously, his slightly tilted face and piercing gaze lead our attention to the blurred background. The blurriness in the image is deliberate, offering a recognizable connection to the real object and subject in the background without rendering it unreal. A man wearing a mask is present within the frame, symbolically tying him to the victims of chemical warfare. For those familiar with its context, the mask serves as a direct visual cue. As the reader becomes immersed in the intense stare of the young boy, the blurred man with the mask

---

[78] Mehdi Monem, *War Victims* (Tehran: Iran Image Productions), 1.

[79] Monem, *War Victims*, 1.

[80] For more on chemical warfare see Firouzkouhi, Mohammedreza et al. "Nurses experiences in chemical emergency departments: Iran-Iraq War, 1980-1988." *International Emergency Nursing* 21, no. 2 (April 2013): 123-128. See also "Medical expert reports use of chemical weapons in Iran-Iraq war." *UN Chronicle* 22, no. 5 (Jan. 1985): 24-26.

also loses depth, condensing everything into a pair of eyes. The photograph becomes an exploration of the eye as the sole point of focus, eclipsing any portrayal of the subjects' mouths or lips and leaving the viewer without the ability to hear spoken words. By intentionally blurring the background, the photograph takes on an abstract quality that combines modern and traditional forms of representation. The modern subject in pain, marginalized and obscured, is transformed into a blurred presence. The photograph allows for the formation of multiple narratives simultaneously: those of the first generation of victims, the second generation of offspring, and the viewer's individual interpretation.

James Young has named the process of the next generation's response to the historical event as "the afterlife of memory, represented in history's after-image: the impressions retained in the mind's eye of a vivid sensation long after the original, external cause has been removed."[81] He suggests that the second generation's narrative is more about their own experience and their own trauma than that of the prior generation. Marianne Hirsch calls the second generation's response to trauma "post-memory," given that it recontextualizes the trauma of the first. There is a compulsive and traumatic repetition that entangles the two together that is mostly about the relationship of the children of trauma survivors to the experiences of their parent(s).[82] In Monem's war photography, trauma is not merely the "afterlife of memory" or "post-memory." Unlike the second and third generations of the Holocaust, whom Young believes experienced the trauma of the first generation mostly through films, photographs, histories, and novels, Monem's second-generation photographic subjects are physically attached to, perplexed, and traumatized by the first generation's tangible trauma and their everyday struggles in life. Cathy Caruth proposes that trauma is an encounter with another, an attempt to tell and listen, listening to another's wound.[83] The look in the boy's eye invites the viewer to an untold story suffocated behind the mask.

Another photograph in this section was taken in 2008 (Figure 1.10) when more than three hundred chemical warfare victims were invited to a clinical recreational gathering along with their families. One victim who could not stand the heavy air of the hotel suddenly collapsed to the ground and was then taken out to the open air. A huge oxygen tank is seen attached to the victim by a plastic tube while his back is to the wall, sitting with one leg bent and the other stretched against the diagonal lines of the cemented ground. His right hand, twisted to reach the left side of his head, exposes his acute condition. The

---

[81] James E. Young, "Toward a Received History of the Holocaust," *History and Theory* 36, no. 4 (December 1997): 23.
[82] Barbie Zelizer, *Visual Culture and the Holocaust* (New Brunswick: Rutgers University Press, 2001), 218.
[83] Caruth, *Unclaimed Experience*, 8.

victim's very young daughter is looking at her father's miserable state right before her eyes, her little hands entangled in front of her in a gesture of bafflement and helplessness. Her face is not clearly visible to the viewer due to the high position of the camera; the viewer looks at the whole scene from above, perhaps from the top floor where all the other attendees are gathered.[84] The high camera angle positions the subject as inferior relative to the viewer's more dominant point of view. The position of the viewer looking at the victim and his daughter enhances the victim's powerless position—his fallen stature, his vulnerability, his body in pain—yet he attracts attention and curiosity. Gunther Kress and Theo van Leeuwen define this positioning of the camera as a visual form of indirect address which represents an offer in which "the viewer is an invisible onlooker and the depicted person is the object of the look – here those depicted either do not know that they are being looked at, […] or act as if they do not know." [85] In this image, the historical past is represented through the post-traumatic life of the survivor and the transgenerational consequences of war through the gaze of offspring. The continuity of traumatic history, the everyday violence of the body in pain, the perpetual suffering, and the detached and unseen position of the bystander, the uninvolved and distant observer: all are framed in this shot. This detachment of the observer from the subject further highlights the unspeakable and incomprehensible nature of the suffering subject that cannot be breached or narrativized. All the subjects, the wounded body, the daughter, and the viewer are isolated in the intense silent entanglement of their frozen and helpless awareness of one other.

Figure 1.10 *Untitled* [taken in Isfahan], Mehdi Monem, 2008, photograph. *War Victims*, 2009.

Courtesy of the artist, Mehdi Monem.

---

[84] Monem, *War Victims*, 101.
[85] Gunther R. Kress and Theo van Leeuwen, *Reading Images: The Grammar of Visual Design* (London: Routledge, 1996), 122.

This paralyzing sense of detachment, the hierarchy of the gaze from above, is perhaps best exemplified in the unveiling of the Iranian monumental statue of the victims of chemical weapons in the Hague (seen in Figure 1.11). Like most paintings of the Iran-Iraq War, the statue depicts a symbolic death. The body of the statue seems to be gradually crumbling to pieces, but here, the deterioration of the body is represented as a tranquil flight to its freedom.[86] For symbolists, the goal is usually not a "complete or even accurate description of visual reality or an idea but the evocation or suggestion of the idea."[87] This form of representation is deemed to be the most suitable platform in which collective anti-colonial or anti-imperial concerns can be represented. In this sense,

> collective traumas are reflections of neither individual suffering nor actual events but symbolic renderings that reconstruct and imagine them, arguments about what must have been and what should be. From the perspective of cultural sociology, the contrast between factual and fictional statements is not an Archimedean point, meaning that the truth of a cultural script depends not on its empirical accuracy but instead on its symbolic power and enactment. But while the trauma process is not rational, it is intentional. It is people who make traumatic meanings in circumstances they have not themselves created and which they do not fully comprehend.[88]

The symbol of the chemical victim's body indirectly references the gradual death of the subject. However, it beatifies and anesthetizes a painful and excruciating experience that is not communicable in simple terms. This statue renders the individual experience of trauma even further invisible and imposes a fictional narrative that constructs a reality detached from empirical truth. Monem's photography, on the other hand, combines elements of the empirical and the real with his artistic vision, which is a commentary on the mythologized version of history as presented by symbolic representation. In this strategy, the traumatic is defined as "the peculiar combination of ordinary and extreme

---

[86] "Berlin, Nov 27, IRNA – A monumental statue titled Chemical Weapons Victims, dedicated by Islamic Republic of Iran to Chemical Weapons Non-Proliferation Organization was unveiled at CWNPO Headquarters in Hague, Netherlands, Monday." "The monument was created by Mr Taher Sheikh-al-Hokamaii, an instructor at the University of Tehran's faculty of fine arts whose works have been exhibited in 17 countries. The monument represents a victim gradually losing his/her life from the effects of chemical weapons whose body is simultaneously converted into peace doves" (OPCW News, web).

[87] "The Symbolist Movement: To Make the Invisible Visible," *Radford University*, http:// www.radford.edu/rbarris/art428/Chapter%202%20Symbolism.html.

[88] Jeffrey C. Alexander, *Trauma: A Social Theory* (Cambridge: Polity, 2012), 4.

elements [that] marks the necessity of considering how the ordinary and extraordinary could interconnect and coexist."[89]

Figure 1.11 "Monument to Victims of Chemical Weapons Unveiled at OPCW Headquarters in the Hague." *The Organization for the Prohibition of Chemical Weapons*, 28 November 2012.

Photo: OPCW.

Continuing his efforts to document the reality of the traumatic consequences of war, another Monem photograph draws our attention to the eyes of a young girl at the center of the camera's focus (Figure 1.12). Two hands coming from behind her – according to the caption, her mother's – are closely placed around her neck. One, a real hand with flesh and bone, is directly positioned on the chest, while the other, a peculiar apparently wax hand, is close to her throat, touching the girl's chin. She is deeply drowned in her mother's arms, who is wearing ornate, native clothing, and she feels the touch of both a human hand of flesh and a cold, soulless artificial hand at the same time. Her gaze into the viewer's eye through the camera lens appears ambiguous – uncertain yet assured by a soft and concealed smile. The artificial hand is an object alluding to the victims of exploding mines, and the gaze demands engagement with a prosthetic hand that seems to be pressing on both, protecting and choking the subject's throat. In a single photograph, the complexity of female subjects is revealed. One aspect portrays a mother who defies institutional expectations by refusing to present her child as a sacrificial offering. Simultaneously, within the same frame, a young girl makes direct eye contact, representing the new generation's defiance of submissive Islamic feminine modesty. These two contrasting expressions within a single photograph encapsulate the multifaceted nature of female experiences.

---

[89] Rothberg, *Traumatic Realism*, 100.

Figure 1.12 *Untitled* [taken in Sar-e Pol-e Zahab], Mehdi Monem, 2007, photograph. *War Victims*, 2009.

Courtesy of the artist, Mehdi Monem.

Kress and van Leeuwen make a distinction in the viewer-text relationship between an "offer" and a "demand": "A gaze of direct address [represents] a demand for the viewer (as the object of the look) to enter into a parasocial relationship with the depicted person."[90] The demand for this direct gaze from an audience is a cry for recognition of the vulnerable groups. In the photograph, the girl, a member of the second generation, represents the continual suffering that follows surviving a traumatic event and the crisis of its aftermath. The war has been over for decades, yet the remaining landmines continue to dismantle lives. The event itself does not belong to the past but instead becomes a perpetual experience that reproduces itself anew. This is made visible through the fragmented body of the mother, who has no face in this frame, yet whose presence is made vivid through her suffocating yet protective entanglement with the child. However, the significant historical "props" in Monem's photography – e.g., oxygen tanks, masks, tubes, artificial body organs – refer to the recent historical trauma, not the seventh-century history of religious identity. Instead of referencing dead subjects as martyrs for a spiritual and redemptive closure, the subjects of his photography are living survivors who experience death a thousand times every day. Unlike the institutional representations of the Iran-Iraq war, which tend to revive the particular collective, mythic aspect of a traumatic past in order to remember and memorialize the conflict, Monem's traumatic realist project of remembrance insists on "confronting the individual voice in a field dominated by political decisions and administrative decrees which

---

[90] Kress and van Leeuwen, *Reading Images*, 122ff.

neutralize the concreteness of despair and death."[91] By documenting the facts of empirical reality, his project provides an alternative point of view, one that demands a departure from the kind of symbolic representations that attempt to "bring total integration" to the post-traumatic lives of those struggling to survive in postwar Iran.

No images could be more poignant in conclusion than those of Mehdi Monem's untitled photograph from Kermanshah (Figure 1.13) and Minoo Emami's *War Painting #15* (Figure 1.14), both depicting explicitly feminine post-war suffering. The subject in Monem's photograph, a victim of a landmine explosion, is portrayed as utterly devastated, burdened with a sense of shame and fragmentation that prevents direct eye contact with the viewer. Her avoidance is different from the females' inward-looking gaze in Kazem Chalipa's paintings. Self-blinded and made anonymous by covering her face, she hides her mutilated body, except the prosthetic leg sticking out from under her black cover, evoking the unavoidable reality of her body in pieces. The hidden figure provokes questioning, a much-anticipated conversation between the viewer and the subject to discover the truth about the experience, about how it felt to be blown up to pieces and yet survive.

Figure 1.13 *Untitled* [taken in Kermanshah], Mehdi Monem, 2001, photograph. *War Victims*, 2009.

Courtesy of the artist, Mehdi Monem.

---

[91] Dominick LaCapra, *Representing the Holocaust: History, Theory, Trauma* (Ithaca: Cornell University Press, 1994), 213.

Figure 1.14 *War Painting #15*, Minoo Emami, *War Collection*, painting, ca. 2008s.

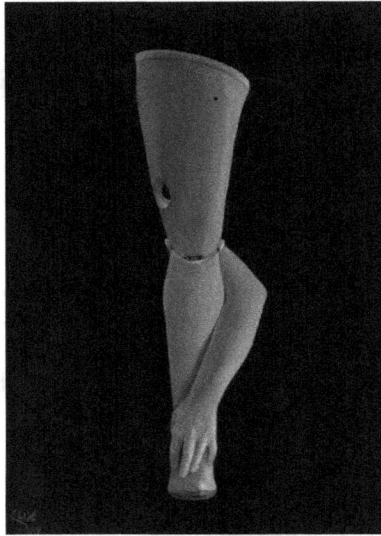

Courtesy of the artist, Minoo Emami.
www.emamiminoo.com

For a female painter like Minoo Emami, whose expressions of war reflect her own experience of living with an amputee veteran of the Iran-Iraq war, the image of a prosthetic leg is compulsively repeated in all her art, reflecting her haunting memory of living with a mutilated body. All her work, however, is devoid of a complete human figure. Years after the death of her husband, her memory of war remains attached to mutilation, and the memory of her relationship with this veteran is suggested by the image of a close embrace in the form of a drained and exhausted gesture of a feminine arm swirled around the prosthetic leg. The position of the fingers evokes a puzzled and helpless female subject in a relationship with a lifeless object. Desire, affection, and compassion all are intertwined with an inanimate object that itself is reminiscent of a brutal past and a difficult present. This fragmentation – the absence of a human figure, a face, and a whole and complete body – represents the physical, emotional, and psychological damage that never ends for a survivor and, to some extent, for the witness, splitting the totality of being a human. Both images remain frozen in a wordless experience, a chilled gesture that only alludes to a strenuous reality.

In this chapter, I have argued that both the physical and psychological aspects of pain resist institutionalized representations that attempt to capture the metaphysical meaning of war. The material reality of war's consequences cannot be assimilated into an anti-imperial/Western framework without disregarding or denying the individual experiences of suffering. The prevailing approach of traumatic realism, as described above, treats war events as objects of knowledge rather than isolating them as spiritual, untouchable moments limited by teleological narratives. Contemporary Iranian filmmakers and photographers have sought to embrace a traumatic realist approach in their work to highlight the enigmatic nature of the survivor's suffering. Their artistic endeavors allow for alternative interpretations to emerge from the collective experience of war. However, unlike these artists, Iranian painters depicting post-traumatic life have yet to explore methods of engaging with viewers and directing their subjects' inward gaze outward to interact with the social, political, and global dimensions of their experiences.

Through my analysis of the progression of postwar Iranian art production, I argue that this outward form of engagement, which attends to diverse personal and individual stories of living with the enduring consequences of violence, is essential in countering the "deadly persistence of religious, racial, and ethnic hatred."[92] This approach also draws significant attention to the social and economic complexities of post-traumatic crises, both on a national and global scale. By demonstrating the shared vulnerability of victims across various wars, incorporating the traumatic real back into representations of the Iran-Iraq War, and allowing cultural practices to reflect on the everyday lives of its victims, we can dismantle the hierarchies and binaries that exist in sanctifying and de-sanctifying death and suffering.

Bibliography

Afary, Janet. *Sexual Politics in Modern Iran.* New York: Cambridge University Press, 2009.

Alexander, Jeffrey C. *Trauma: A Social Theory.* Cambridge: Polity, 2012.

Apel, Dora. *Memory Effects: The Holocaust and the Art of Secondary Witnessing.* New Brunswick: Rutgers University Press, 2002.

Caruth, Cathy. *Unclaimed Experience: Trauma, Narrative, and History.* Baltimore: Johns Hopkins University Press, 1996.

Craven, Catherine. "How the Visual Arts Can Further the Cause of Human Rights," *E-International Relations,* 27 October 2011. https://www.e-ir.info/2011/10/27/the-visual-arts-and-the-cause-of-human-rights-in-dealing-with-suffering-and-trauma/.

Crockett, Dennis. "The Most Famous Painting of the 'Golden Twenties'? Otto Dix and the Trench Affair." *Art Journal* 51, no. 1, 1992: 72-80.

Davari, Arash. "A Return to Which Self?: 'Ali Shari'Ati and Frantz Fanon on the Political Ethics of Insurrectionary Violence." *Comparative Studies of South Asia, Africa and the Middle East* 34, no. 1 (2014): 86–105.

---

[92] Rothberg, *Traumatic Realism,* 272.

Dowd, Maureen. "Powell Without Picasso." *The New York Times*, 5 February 2003. https://www.nytimes.com/2003/02/05/opinion/powell-without-picas so.html.

Ebrahim Hatamikia, director. *From Karkheh to Rhein*[93] (1992; Tehran: Siva Film), DVD.

Egan, Eric. *The Films of Makhmalbaf: Cinema, Politics & Culture in Iran.* Washington, D.C.: Mage Publishers, 2005.

Esfandiary, Shahab. *Iranian Cinema and Globalization: National, Transnational and Islamic Dimensions.* Bristol: Intellect, 2012.

Fanon, Frantz (auth.) and Richard Philcox (trans.). *The Wretched of the Earth.* Translated by Richard Philcox. New York: Grove Press, 1977.

Gassier, Pierre, Juliet Wilson Bareau, and Franc ois Lachenal. *The Life and Complete Works of Francisco Goya.* New York: Reynal and Morrow, 1971.

Ghodrati. Maryam, Personal Interview with Morteza Goodarzi Dibaj, 20 August 2014.

Goodarzi Dibaj, Morteza. *Committed Social and Religious Art in Iran: Paintings of Revolution.* Tehran: Farhangestan e Honar Publication, 2009.

Halaka, John. "Artist Statement," *John Halaka.* http://johnhalaka.com/artists tatements.html.

Kress, Gunther R., and Theo van Leeuwen. *Reading Images: The Grammar of Visual Design. London:* Routledge, 1996.

LaCapra, Dominick. *Representing the Holocaust: History, Theory, Trauma.* Ithaca: Cornell University Press, 1994.

Lifton, Robert Jay. *Death in Life. [Electronic Resource]: Survivors of Hiroshima.* Chapel Hill, NC: University of North Carolina Press, 1991.

McSorley, Kevin. *War and the Body: Militarisation, Practice and Experience.* New York: Routledge, 2013.

Mitchell, Jolyon P. *Promoting Peace, Inciting Violence: The Role of Religion and Media.* New York: Routledge, 2012.

Mohsen Makhmalbaf, director. *Marriage of the Blessed* (1989; Tehran: Ferdosi Multimedia). DVD.

Monem, Mehdi. *War Victims.* Tehran: Iran Image Publications, 2009.

"Monument to Victims of Chemical Weapons Unveiled at OPCW Headquarters in The Hague." *Organization for the Prohibition of Chemical Weapons (OPCW)*, 28 November 2012. https://www.opcw.org/media-centre/news/20 12/11/monument-victims-chemical-weapons-unveiled-opcw-headquarters -hague.

Muther, Richard, et al. *The History of Modern Painting.* New York: Henry Holt and Co., 1895.

Nayar, K. Pramod. *Contemporary Literary and Cultural Theory: From Structuralism to Ecocriticism.* London: Pearson Education India, 2009.

"A New Battle of Karbala." *The Graphics of Revolution and War: Iranian Poster Arts.* Chicago: The Hanna Holborn Gray Special Collections Research Center at the University of Chicago Library (exhibition on view 15 October to

---

[93] *From Karkheh to Rhein* (Ebrahim Hatamikia, 1992) - از کرخه تا راین

18 December 2011). https://www.lib.uchicago.edu/collex/exhibits/graphic s-revolution-and-war-iranian-poster-arts/new-battle-karbala/.

Rosenblum, Robert. "Picasso's Disasters of War: The Art of Blasphemy." In *Picasso and the War Years 1937-1945*: 39-53. Edited by Pablo Picasso. London: Thames and Hudson, 1998.

Rothberg, Michael. "Decolonizing Trauma Studies: A Response." *Studies in the Novel* 40, no. 1- 2, 2008: 224-234.

——. *Multidirectional Memory: Remembering the Holocaust in an Age of Decolonization*. Redwood City: Stanford University Press, 2009.

——. *Traumatic Realism: The Demands of Holocaust Representation*. Minneapolis: University of Minnesota Press, 2000.

Sassoon, Siegfried. *The Complete Memoirs of George Sherston*. Chicago: World Book, Inc., 1940.

Scarry, Elaine. *The Body in Pain: The Making and Unmaking of the World*. New York: Oxford University Press, 1985.

Schwab, Gabriele. "Writing Against Memory and Forgetting." *Literature and Medicine* 25, no. 1, 2006: 95–121.

Schweizer, Harold. *Suffering and the Remedy of Art*. Albany: State University of New York Press, 1997.

Shields, David. *War Is Beautiful: The New York Times Pictorial Guide to the Glamour of Armed Conflict*. New York: PowerHouse Books, 2015.

Söderbäck, Fanny. "Revolutionary Time: Revolt as Temporal Return." *Signs* 37, no. 2, 2012: 301-324.

Sontag. Susan. *Regarding the Pain of Others*. New York: Farrar, Straus and Giroux, 2003.

"The Symbolist Movement: To Make the Invisible Visible." *Radford University*, http://www.radford.edu/rbarris/art428/Chapter%202%20Symbolism.html.

Talebi, Shahla. "From the Light of the Eyes to the Eyes of the Power: State and Dissident Martyrs in Post-Revolutionary Iran." *Visual Anthropology* 25, no. i-ii, 2012: 120-147.

Young, James E. "Toward a Received History of the Holocaust." *History and Theory* 36, no. 4 (December 1997): 21-43.

——. *The Stages of Memory: Reflections on Memorial Art, Loss, and the Spaces Between*. Amherst: University of Massachusetts Press, 2016.

Zelizer, Barbie. *Visual Culture and the Holocaust*. New Brunswick: Rutgers University Press, 2001.

Further Reading

Abrahamian, Ervand. *Iran Between Two Revolutions*. Princeton: Princeton University Press, 1982.

Ankori, Gannit. *Palestinian Art*. London: Reaktion, 2006.

Apolinar, Lydia. "Ali Shariati: Ideologue of the Iranian Revolution." *Cosmonaut, Inc.* 29 November 2019. https://cosmonaut.blog/2019/11/29/ali-shariati-ide ologue-of-the-iranian-revolution/.

Bombardier, Alice, and Nasser Palangi. "War Painting and Pilgrimage in Iran." *Visual Anthropology* 25, iss. i-ii (Jan. 2012): 148–166.

Bombardier, Alice. "Iranian Revolutionary Painting on Canvas: Iconographic Study on the Martyred Body." *Iranian Studies: Journal of the International Society for Iranian Studies* 46, no. 4 (July 2013): 583–600.

Caruth, Cathy. "Trauma and Experience: Introduction." In *Trauma: Explorations in Memory*, 3-13. Edited by Cathy Caruth. Baltimore: Johns Hopkins University Press, 1995.

Chelkowski, Peter J., and Hamid Dabashi. *Staging a Revolution: The Art of Persuasion in the Islamic Republic of Iran*. New York: New York University Press, 1999.

Firouzkouhi, Mohammedreza et al. "Nurses experiences in chemical emergency departments: Iran-Iraq War, 1980-1988." *International Emergency Nursing* 21, no. 2 (April 2013): 123-128.

Forward, Roy. "Beauty, Truth and Goodness in Dix's War." *NGA, National Gallery of Australia*. Accessed November 5, 2019. https://nga.gov.au/dix/.

Haines, D.D. and S.C. Fox. "Acute and Long-Term Impact of Chemical Weapons: Lessons from the Iran-Iraq War." *Forensic Science Review* 26, no. 2 (July 2014): 97-114.

Karcher, Eva. *Otto Dix*. Translated by John Ormrod. New York: Crown Publishers, Inc., 1987.

Khorrami, Mohammad Mehdi. "Narratives of Silence: Persian Fiction of the 1980-1988 Iran-Iraq War." In *Moments of Silence: Authenticity in the Cultural Expressions of the Iran-Iraq War, 1980-1988*: 217-235. Edited by Arta Khakpour et al. New York: New York University Press, 2016.

Khosronejad, Pedram. *Iranian Sacred Defence Cinema: Religion, Martyrdom and National Identity*. Canon Pyon: Sean Kingston Publishing, 2012.

LaCapra, Dominick. *Writing History, Writing Trauma*. Baltimore: Johns Hopkins University Press, 2001.

Leighten, Patricia. "Response: Artists in Times of War." *Art Bulletin* 91, no. 1, 2009: 35-44.

"Medical expert reports the use of chemical weapons in Iran-Iraq war." *UN Chronicle* 22, no. 5 (Jan. 1985): 24-26.

Naficy, Hamid. Vol. 1-4 of *A Social History of Iranian Cinema*. Durham: Duke University Press, 2011-2012.

Saramifar, Younes. "Framing the War in the Post-War Era: Exploring the Counter-Narratives in Frames of an Iranian War Photographer Thirty Years After the Ceasefire with Iraq. "*Media, War & Conflict* 12, no. 4 (Dec. 2019): 392-410.

"Skat Players." *Utopia/Dystopia, Examining Art of the WWI Era*. Spring 2012. https://utopiadystopiawwi.wordpress.com/new-objectivity/otto-dix/skat-players/.

Suler, John. *Photographic Psychology: Image and Psyche*. Web, True Center Publishing. Accessed 6 January 2018, http://truecenterpublishing.com/photopsy/camera_angles.htm.

Vallen, Mark. "Simon Schama's the Power of Art." *Mark Vallen's Art for a Change*, 18 June 2007. http://art-for-a-change.com/blog/2007/06/simon-schamas-power-of-art.html.

Young, James E. "Regarding the Pain of Women: Questions of Gender and the Arts of Holocaust Memory." *PMLA* 124, no. 5 (October 2009): 1778-1786.

Chapter 2

Regarding the Pain of Women: Gender and the Arts of Holocaust Memory[1]

James E. Young

University of Massachusetts Amherst

Abstract

The visual and literary depictions of Jewish women's suffering during the Holocaust often tend to objectify women's bodies and obfuscate their psychological pain and voices. We have finally begun to amass a large and profound critical literature on gender and the Holocaust, which, alongside Sontag's work on photography, might help us look at how and why the public gaze of photographers, curators, historians, and museumgoers continues to turn women into objects of memory, idealized casts of perfect suffering and victimization, and even emblems of larger Jewish suffering during the Holocaust. This chapter explores our relation to these hardened idealizations of women in the arts of Holocaust memory, for in "regarding the pain of women," we often split these women off from their lives and deaths, their stories and experiences through the writing of Anne Frank, Irene Eber, and Chaim Nachman Bialik, and the artwork of Art Spiegelman, David Levinthal, and Gerhard Richter, among others.

Keywords*:* Holocaust, art, photography, objectification, sexuality, Nazism, symbolism

* * *

My title is a deliberate variation on Susan Sontag's *Regarding the Pain of Others.* I mean this both as an homage to Sontag and as an extension of her searing critique of war photography and its reflexive objectification of suffering, its conversion of victims into *objets d'art.*[2] But why, in particular, the pain of women Holocaust victims here? Because we have finally begun to amass a large and profound critical literature on gender and the Holocaust, which, alongside

---

[1] This chapter is an adaptation of the third chapter from my previous work *The Stages of Memory: Reflections on Memorial Art, Loss, and the Spaces Between*, published in 2016 by University of Massachusetts Press.

[2] Susan Sontag, *Regarding the Pain of Others* (New York: Farrar, Straus, Giroux, 2003).

Sontag's work on photography, might now help us look at how and why the public gaze of photographers, curators, historians, and museum-goers continues to turn women into objects of memory, idealized casts of perfect suffering and victimization, even as emblematic of larger Jewish suffering during the Holocaust.

Here, I would like to explore our relationship to these hardened idealizations of women in the arts of Holocaust memory, for I have found that in "regarding the pain of women," we often split these women off from their own lives and deaths, their own stories and experiences. We may hold the pain of women in high regard, perhaps. However, when we regard it, we also find spectacle in it, converting their suffering into cultural, even psychological objects around which we tell our own stories, find large meanings, fixed and full of symbolic portent. As a result, particular parts of women's experiences as women remain unexpressed, unregarded, and even negated. Moreover, as objects in museums necessarily fix otherwise fluid and changing life into emblematic illustrations of their explanatory theses, I find that these idealized icons of victimization, innocence, or even resistance come to substitute for the stories women might be telling about themselves. They serve as fixed objects around which other survivors' stories are told, around which cultures and nations may even tell their own stories. However, there are stories about women in the Holocaust, and there are stories the women have to tell. Too often, our stories about these women have left no space for the stories women have to tell, stories that seem to have no place in the fixed field of the Holocaust canon.

The problem is that the actual experiences of women – as told by themselves – are often converted almost immediately on being regarded into symbolic significance or are hardly regarded at all. Feelings of helplessness, vulnerability, and physical torment are often masked immediately by the icon of resistance, heroism, or martyrdom (think of the photograph of Marusia Bruskina being hanged as a partisan in Minsk (Figure 2.1), of Hannah Senesh as a heroic paratrooper, or of Anne Frank as a universal beacon of hope, according to her father Otto Frank's protective editing of his daughter's diary). Once objectified, the pain of these women assumes iconic proportions, which is to say, a completely over-determined meaning. Though the scholarship of numerous critics and historians has effectively de-bunked the taboo of gender-based study of the Holocaust, the absence of women's voices and their experiences as women is still all too emblematic of the ways gender and sexuality have been split off from Holocaust history and memory.[3]

---

[3] Among other ground-breaking works, see Dalia Ofer and Lenore J. Weitzman, Eds. *Women in the Holocaust* (New Haven and London: Yale University Press, 1998); Carol Rittner and John K. Roth, Eds. *Different Voices: Women and the Holocaust* (New York: Paragon House, 1993); Myrna Goldenberg and E. Baer, Eds. *Experience and Expression: Women and the*

The question is: do we actually ever see the pain of women, or do we see only our reflections in the shiny veneer of women as symbols of resistance, innocence, and regeneration? Toward what end do we regard, represent, or even reproduce the pain of women in the Holocaust? To show how evil the Nazi killers were? To show how innocent the victims were? To strive to abolish such suffering altogether, as Susan Sontag would suggest?[4] To the extent that all photographs objectify, in Sontag's words, turning their subjects into objects that can then be owned and made meaningful by those who "own" them, how should we now regard them?

Figure 2.1 The execution by hanging of Masha Bruskina and Volodya Sherbateyvich.

The German execution of Mariya (Masha) Bruskina in Minsk on October 26, 1941. Referred to officially in Soviet texts as "the unknown girl," she was remembered for decades after the war as a seventeen-year-old Soviet Communist partisan who helped injured Soviet soldiers escape hospital captivity. She was identified in the 1960s by name and as a Jewish member of the Minsk resistance. In 2009, she was identified on a plaque near the site of her execution as M. B. Bruskina, hanged as a Soviet patriot by the Fascists. Eventually, a monument was erected in her honor in Kfar Hayarok in Israel, and a street was named after her in Jerusalem. *Photo: The execution by hanging of Masha Bruskina and Volodya Sherbateyvich by an officer with the 707th Infantry Division. United States Holocaust Memorial Museum Photo Archives # 25136. Courtesy of Ada Dekhtyar. Copyright of United States Holocaust Memorial Museum.*

As Jews were culled from the general population for "special handling" by the Nazis, Jewish women were further singled out from among Jewish prisoners for a

---

Holocaust (Detroit: Wayne State University Press, 2003); Esther Katz and Joan Ringelheim, Eds. *Proceedings of the Conference on Women Surviving: The Holocaust* (New York: Institute for Research in History, 1983); Miriam Peskowitz and Laura Levitt, Eds. *Judaism since Gender* (New York and London: Routledge, 1997); Esther Fuchs, Ed. *Women and the Holocaust: Narrative and Representation* (Lanham and Oxford: University Press of America, 1999); Marlene E. Heinemann, *Gender and Destiny: Women Writers and the Holocaust* (New York and Westport: Greenwood Press, 1986); and Sara R. Horowitz, *Gender, Genocide, and Jewish Memory* (2000).

[4] Susan Sontag, *Regarding the Pain of Others* (New York: Farrar, Straus, Giroux, 2003), 8.

kind of "priority" special handling. As the bearers of the next generation of Jews, they were murdered as Jews and women, as biological carriers of the Jewish race. As Jews were singled out for total annihilation, the women among the Jews were singled out to be killed first and in greater numbers and proportions than men, for reasons articulated most chillingly by the Nazi leadership itself. In the words of Heinrich Himmler, women were to be accorded special treatment, that is, killed without delay, in order to "obliterate the biological basis of Jewry." As described in the Wannsee Protocol, women and children had to be killed in order to eliminate "the germ cell of a new Jewish revival." Alternatively, in the words of Otto Six of the RSHA, to "deprive Jewry of its biological reserves." It was with all this in mind that Himmler elaborated on what he called the "logic" of killing women and children during the Einsatzgruppen actions in the East:

> When I was forced in some village to act against partisans and Jewish Commissars... then as a principal I gave the order to kill the women and children of those partisans and Commissars, too... Believe me, that order was not so easy to carry out as it was logically thought out and can be stated in this hall. However, we must constantly recognize what kind of primitive, primordial, natural race struggle we are engaged in.

> We came to the question: what about the women and children? I have decided to find a clear solution here, too. In fact, I did not regard myself as justified in exterminating the men [only], while letting avengers in the shape of children... grow up. The difficult decision had to be taken to make these people disappear from the face of the earth.[5]

That is, built into the Nazi genocide of the Jews was the gender-specific mass murder of Jewish women, deemed the procreators of the Jewish race, a predicate of the genocide. In fact, this is where, I believe, gender and sexuality are split off together from the larger history of the Holocaust, from the larger reservoir of collected memory. Whereas women's sexuality played a paramount role in both the Nazis' rationale for their mass murder and in the specific ways women were degraded, humiliated, and violated as women, there was almost no parallel experience in the stories of Jewish men at the hands of their captors. Men and women shared stories of resistance, deprivation, pain, starvation, deportation, separation from families, and mass murder. However, they did not share stories of sexual exploitation, violations of religious modesty and decorum,

---

[5] In Bradley F. Smith and Agnes F. Peterson, Eds. *Heinrich Himmler: Geheimreden, 1933 bis 1945* (Frankfurt: Propylaen, 1974), p. 201, p. xxx, as quoted in Joan Ringelheim, "Genocide and Gender: A Split Memory," paper delivered at "Memory and the second World War in International Comparative Perspective," Amsterdam, April 26-28, 1995. The earlier citations by Otto Six, the Wannsee Protocol, and Himmler are also drawn from this paper, which cites *Trials of War Criminals* (Nuremberg Green Series), vol. 4, p. 525 as their source.

rape, child-birth, or abortions – none of which had a place in traditional histories of the Holocaust until pioneers like Joan Ringelheim pointed out what she called the "split between gender and genocide."[6]

Just as starvation, beatings, and dehumanization were part of all the prisoners' experiences, so were rape, threats of rape, sexual humiliation, and childbirth, also part of the female victims' experiences. Without a place or conceptual framework for such memory, as Ringelheim suggests, these experiences are almost never voiced.[7] In fact, it is often this voicelessness itself that endures as a theme in art and writing about the Holocaust.

Sometimes, as in the case of Pauline, from Joan Ringelheim's early oral archives, it is the survivor who splits the sexual abuse she suffered during the Holocaust (in hiding, in this particular case) from what she came to regard after the war as "acceptable" Holocaust history. After relating in uncomfortable detail instances of being molested by the men and boys who were also hiding her from the Nazis, Pauline asked her interviewer, Joan Ringelheim, a question: "[In light] of what happened, [what] we suffered and saw – the humiliation in the ghetto, seeing our relatives dying and taken away... seeing the ghetto burn and seeing people jumping out and burned – is this [sexual abuse] important?" Alternatively, as Ringelheim asked, "Was this part of her story also a part of the Holocaust story?" Ringelheim answers aptly, I think, that for Pauline and many other women, memory itself had been split between "traditional versions of Holocaust history and her own experience."[8]

However, in other cases, it is the readers and editors of a work, like Anne Frank's diary, who do the splitting for their related reasons. "The Diary of a Young Girl," as the world came to know Anne Frank's diary from the annex in the early and mid-fifties, was, in fact, the literary creation of a devoted and grief-stricken father trying to salvage universal meaning from his daughter's death in Bergen-Belsen.[9] As a loving and protective father who could not ultimately protect his family from the wrath of the Nazis, Otto Frank finally sought to protect all that remained of his second daughter – i.e., her image, her diary – from all impertinent readings, editing out all references to fights with her mother, her sexual awakening, her own grave and profound doubts about her

---

[6] See Joan Ringelheim, "The Split between Gender and the Holocaust," in Ofer and Weitzman, Eds. *Women in the Holocaust*. For an earlier iteration of this, see Ringelheim's, "The Unethical and the Unspeakable: Women and the Holocaust," *Simon Wiesenthal Center Annual*, Volume 1 (1984).

[7] Ibid., 342.

[8] Ibid., 343, 344.

[9] First published in Holland as *Het Achterhuis* (or The Annex), it appeared as *Anne Frank: The Diary of a Young Girl*, translated from the Dutch by B.M. Mooyaart-Doubleday, with an Introduction of Eleanor Roosevelt (Garden City, N.Y.: Doubleday & Company, 1952).

fate. In effect, his preservation of her memory and her diary was inseparable from the solace and hope he needed to find in her memory and diary. Otto's version ensured that the diary of a young woman coming of age would remain "the diary of a young girl" – his little girl, whom he could not protect but whose memory he protected so ferociously.

As the unexpurgated, critical edition of Anne Frank's diary reveals, the early published version of the diary, as well as stage and film spin-offs, were less historical documents of Anne's subjectivity and more the testament to the universal values of hope and tolerance idealized by Anne's father.[10] Unlike, say, Ruth Kluger's unremittingly frank remembrance of her own "Holocaust girlhood,"[11] a period of intense feelings for and conflict with her mother and father, there was no space in Otto Frank's story of his daughter for the parts of her subjectivity, her story, which did not accord with his highly-idealized remembrance of his family and his own need to fix her diary as a beacon of hope. There was also no place for Anne's early sexualization in her father's nonsexual remembrance of her. However, it is also true that Otto merely did for Anne what many female survivors often did for themselves. In Joan Ringelheim's terms, he split off her necessarily gendered experiences from the universally idealized notion of her martyrdom. In Otto's case, it may also have been a matter of splitting off Anne's sexual experiences from the rest of her reflections as a way to preserve, even instantiate, the ideal of the pre-sexualized child as an innocent victim, an image meant to stand in for the innocence of all Jewish victims.

Nor is Otto Frank the only father and husband in the literature to substitute his story for that of a lost loved one. Indeed, some of the most interesting portrayals of women are the "missing" or absent voices of women and their stories, the ways they are either blocked or expurgated, shown as missing – thereby assigning significance to the silence or absence. In *Maus: A Survivor's Tale*, Art Spiegelman shows both the voicelessness of his mother and the ways he and his father have collaborated to fill her absence with their own words – the ways his father would, in speaking about her, also presume to speak for her. Having destroyed her notebooks in a fit of grief and sadness, Spiegelman's father, Vladek, would now fill the space left behind with his own story.[12] In fact,

---

[10] In effect, the unexpurgated diary has even served to counterpoint some of the universal and national myths that brought the Anne Frank House and Museum into being and which continue to sustain it. See *The Diary of Anne Frank: The Critical Edition* (New York: Doubleday, 1989). Also see James E. Young, "The Anne Frank House: Holland's Memorial Shrine of the Book," in Hyman A. Enzer and Sandra Solotaroff-Enzer, Eds. *Anne Frank: Reflections on Her Life and Legacy* (Urbana and Chicago: University of Illinois Press, 2000): 223-228.

[11] See Ruth Kluger, *Still Alive: A Holocaust Girlhood Remembered* (New York: The Feminist Press of the City University of New York, 2001).

[12] Art Spiegelman, *Maus: A Survivor's Tale* (New York: Pantheon, 1986, 1991), 158.

Art's own story might even be said to begin literally on the premise of his mother's missing and longed-for voice. Where should Vladek begin his story? He asks his son. "Start with Mom," Art coaxes.[13] The entire subsequent co-telling is basically structured around the missing mother, as Nancy Miller has pointed out. And then, by making the recovery of the story itself a visible part of *Maus*, Spiegelman can also hint darkly at the story not being recovered here; the ways that telling one story always leaves another untold. In Spiegelman's case, this deep, unrecoverable story is his mother's memory of her experiences during the Holocaust.

Vladek cannot volunteer this story. It takes Artie to ask what Anja was doing all this time. "Housework... and knitting... reading... and she was writing always in her diary," Vladek answers. The diaries did not survive the war, Vladek says, but she did write her memoirs afterward. "Ohmigod! Where are they? I need those for this book!" Artie exclaims.[14] Instead of answering, Vladek coughs and asks Artie to stop smoking. It is making him short of breath. What seems to be a mere interruption turns out to be a prescient delaying tactic. Vladek had, after all, burned Anja's memoirs in a fit of grief after her suicide. Was it the memory of smoke from the burned memoirs or Artie's cigarettes that now made him short of breath?

At the end of the first volume, Spiegelman depicts the moment at which his father admits not only destroying his mother's memoirs but leaving them unread. "Murderer," the son mutters. Here, he seems to realize that Anja's lost story haunts his father's entire story. However, worse, it dawns on the son that his entire project may itself be premised on the destruction of his mother's memoirs, their displacement and violation. "I will tell it for her," says the father.[15] Spiegelman does not attempt to retell Anja's story at all but leaves it known only by its absence; he is an accomplice to the usurpation of his dead mother's voice. It is a blank page to be presented as blank. Nancy Miller has suggested, profoundly: "It is as if at the heart of *Maus*'s dare is the wish to save the mother by retrieving her narrative; as if the comic book version of Auschwitz were the son's normalization of another impossible reality: restoring the missing word, the Polish notebooks."[16] As a void at the heart of *Maus*, the mother's lost story may be *Maus*'s negative center of gravity, the invisible planet around which both the father's telling and Spiegelman's recovery revolve.

---

[13] Ibid., 12.
[14] Ibid., 84.
[15] Ibid., 158.
[16] Nancy Miller, "Cartoons of the Self: Portrait of the Artist as a Young Murderer: Art Spiegelman's Maus," 49.

Moreover, as was the case for Otto Frank, Vladek's inability to protect his first child, Richieu, who died in hiding, is literally unspeakable. The result is a fixed image, a photograph, of his murdered child as a perfect victim in the father's version of the story. It is the preservation of objectified memory when life itself cannot be preserved. The unspeakability of male helplessness is both relieved by and expressed in both Otto's and Vladek's objectification of even their own loved ones as perfectly idealized victims.

Neither is the propensity to fix such idealizations limited to self-expurgated or father-expurgated narratives. Several widely circulated images of women being attacked, which were taken by the Nazis themselves, have also begun to assume a certain canonical (i.e., fixed) status in museums and illustrated histories of the Holocaust. I refer here specifically to photographs taken by S.S. photographers on the eastern front: one of a woman cradling a child and whirling away from a Nazi rifleman aiming at her near Ivangorod, Ukraine, in 1942 (Figure 2.2) and the other of a group of women, forced to strip naked before being marched to the shooting pits outside of Liepaja, Latvia in December 1941.[17] In the first image's recirculation and exhibition in museums (including Yad Vashem and the U.S. Holocaust Memorial Museum, among others), we find that this Nazi photograph has itself become part of the iconic currency of the Holocaust – and has thus taken on a life of its own. Beyond its status as a Nazi artifact, it resonates with a conglomerate of axiomatic truisms so that the image has become emblematic of killers and victims: the woman and child represent the vulnerability and blamelessness of the victims, the generations of Jewish life that would be wiped out in a single blow, a grotesque pieta in which both mother and child are both murdered, a certain sacrifice.

The resonances of the second image, however, play out much differently. As it echoes, however faintly, an area in which artists are practically forbidden to tread – i.e., the sexuality of victims, the possible sado-sexuality of the killers. The taboo on this subject explains why so many, including myself, had trouble assimilating images from David Levinthal's series of staged Polaroid photographs from *Mein Kampf* of crematoria stuffed with bodies of women in glaringly sexual poses. Here, too, I have been forced to revisit some of my strong objections to what I regarded as a deliberate eroticization of the murder process. I even tried to talk the artist into eliding from the exhibition several images of naked Japanese dolls with gaudy red nipples. As I voiced my qualms, the artist responded that Art Spiegelman had also tried to talk him out of showing these particular images. I remember telling the artist, "Nowhere in the literature have

---

[17] Though often reproduced, they can be seen most clearly in the museum catalogue, Ella Gutterman and Avner Shalev, Eds. *To Bear Witness: Holocaust Remembrance at Yad Vashem* (Jerusalem: Yad Vashem Publications, 2005), pp. 126, 114 respectively.

I found anything to suggest an erotic component to the killing process," that I had encountered it "only in the imaginations of those who weren't there," like D.M. Thomas in his novel, *The White Hotel*, or William Styron in *Sophie's Choice*. Now I realize that I was missing the point, that both Spiegelman and I had reflexively split off an aspect of the killing that we had difficulty assimilating.

Figure 2.2 Iconic image of woman and child being shot by SS gunman in Ivanhorod, Ukraine, 1942.

Photo: German police take aim at Jews from Ivanhorod who have just finished preparing their own grave. United States Holocaust Memorial Museum Photo Archives. Courtesy of Jerzy Tomaszewski. Public Domain.

The resonances of the second image, however, play out much differently. As it echoes, however faintly, an area in which artists are practically forbidden to tread – i.e., the sexuality of victims, the possible sado-sexuality of the killers. The taboo on this subject explains why so many, including myself, had trouble assimilating images from David Levinthal's series of staged Polaroid photographs from *Mein Kampf* of crematoria stuffed with bodies of women in glaringly sexual poses. Here, too, I have been forced to revisit some of my strong objections to what I regarded as a deliberate eroticization of the murder process. I even tried to talk the artist into eliding from the exhibition several images of naked Japanese dolls with gaudy red nipples. As I voiced my qualms, the artist responded that Art Spiegelman had also tried to talk him out of showing these particular images. I remember telling the artist, "Nowhere in the literature have I found anything to suggest an erotic component to the killing process," that I had encountered it "only in the imaginations of those who weren't there," like D.M. Thomas in his novel, *The White Hotel*, or William Styron in *Sophie's Choice*. Now I realize that I was missing the point, that both Spiegelman and I had reflexively split off an aspect of the killing that we had difficulty assimilating.

David Levinthal replied on two levels, which took a few moments to sink in. First, he said, whether or not there was actually a sexual, erotic component to the murder process, it remains certainly – if unfortunately – true that in many of its popular representations, the Holocaust has been eroticized, whether we like it or not. Since his subject was not "what happened" but rather our culture's hyper-mediated simulations of the Holocaust, he was attempting to show a Holocaust porno-kitsch already at play in the cultural transformations of these terrible scenes. In popular movies like Steven Spielberg's *Schindler's List* or Liliana Cavani's *The Night Porter,* or novels like D.M. Thomas's *The White Hotel,* for example, Eros and Thanatos are twinned as constituent elements of Holocaust victimization, projected reflexively onto victims by a culture obsessed with both, a culture that has long linked the two as fatally interconnected – a culture that has eventually grown dependent on their union for commercial and entertainment success.[18] Rather than ignoring them, Levinthal made a place, however ambiguous it may seem, for what Georges Bataille has described as the dual impulses underpinning our gaze, "desire and violence."[19]

This I could swallow, if with some difficulty. But it was Levinthal's second, implied proposition here that flew in the face of all that I then considered conventional wisdom. That is, he believed that both killers and victims understood that part of the dehumanization of the Jews included their sexual degradation in the moments before death – that part of the violence against the Jews, notable by its absence in survivor literature, he believed, was the sexual abuse of women, their manhandling by the Nazis during the killing process. Was this something he knew that I didn't know? As it turns out, it was.[20]

As women have been objectified in these toys and the Jews were objectified by the Nazis, the victims would here be presented as objectified twice over. Designed as sexual objects, to begin with, the artist's Japanese dolls are used to recapitulate not only the relationship between killers and victims but also, if more implicitly, that between contemporary viewers and these very images. With them, Levinthal suggests that with every representation of their murder, the Jews are, in some sense, murdered again and again. Robbed of life by the Nazi gunmen, the victims are robbed of their dignity by the observing photographer – and then again with the recirculation of such images. Only now are we the passive bystanders, and maybe not all so innocent at that.

At least part of what makes these images so unnerving for viewers is their suggestion that we, as viewers, maybe no less complicit in the continuing degradation of the victim than the original Nazi photographer. Another

---

[18] For an elaboration of the ways women's corpses, in particular, have been represented as emblematic in our culture, see Elisabeth Bronfen, *Over Her Dead Body: Configurations of Femininity, Death & the Aesthetic* (New York: Routledge Press, 1992).

[19] Georges Bataille, *Eroticism* (London: J. Calder, 1962).

[20] A few months later, in April 1995, at a conference in Amsterdam on "Memory and the Second World War in International Perspective," Joan Ringelheim gave me a copy of her paper on "Genocide and Gender: A Split Memory," a version of which was later printed in Dalia Ofer and Lenore Weitzman's collection on *Women in the Holocaust* (see above).

calculatedly disturbing image in this series is Levinthal's formal design and composition that foists this realization upon viewers, leaving little room to escape such conclusions. In this work, four women (portrayed by sexy dolls with porcelain white skin) are being shot by two S.S. gunmen. Their rifles aim into a perspective vortex at the center of the image: we look over the shoulders of both gunmen right into the center of the V. Three women have their arms up as if to ward off the bullets, and one woman is already falling. Only the muzzle of one of the rifles is in focus, though the colors of bodies are bright and sharp, a swirl of whites, blues, and gun-metal gray, all tinged by red smoke and glare.

From our vicarious but central vantage point, we too are implicated in this shooting – as is the photographer, who seems passively to be watching the scene, a participant inspired by the S.S. photographers who recorded but did not prevent similar shootings. As Susan Sontag has made so painfully explicit, "Photography is essentially an art of non-intervention... The person who intervenes cannot record; the person who is recording cannot intervene."[21] That is, even as a passive spectator, the photographer plays a role, if by default, in the events he would capture: to some extent, every photographer is both a choreographer of the event and a representative of it. In the case of Levinthal's image, which he has literally choreographed before shooting, such a truism is made palpable. By forcing us to view the shooting from a vantage point between the two gunmen, the artist has, in effect, made us the implied third gun.

The complicated role such images play in the public sphere came into especially sharp relief in a slightly different context a few years ago in Jerusalem. As visitors entered the former public plaza at Israel's National Holocaust Memorial Museum, Yad Vashem, they came upon a full-scale reproduction of Nathan Rapoport's Warsaw Ghetto Monument, book-like opened, front and back now stands side-by-side. In a further modification of the original in Warsaw, the Liberté figure's right breast was covered modestly, a respectful gesture to Jerusalem's religious community. Rapoport's heroic *Liberté* icon is meant to lead, no victim. For images of the victims, visitors entering the historical galleries of the old museum found themselves face to face with wall-sized photographs depicting the Jewish women of Liepaja stripped, naked, shivering in fear, staring back at the German photographer's lens as he shot their picture moments before his cohort shot these women dead (Figure 2.3). When confronted by leaders of the ultra-Orthodox community in Jerusalem, the curators at Yad Vashem refused to remove wall-sized photographs taken by the Nazis of naked Jewish women on their way to the killing pits in Latvia (many of them orthodox, their strict codes of sexual modesty violated unequivocally by the S.S. photographer). The museum replied that because this degradation, too, was part of the reality of

---

[21] Susan Sontag, *On Photography* (New York: Farrar, Straus, and Giroux, Inc., 1973), 11-12.

the Holocaust, it had to be shown as part of the historical record – whether or not it offended the religious community's rigorous sense of modesty. In the eyes of the religious community, however, the humiliation and violation of these women's modesty was as much a part of the crime as their eventual murder. That these murdered women's modesty would be violated yet again by museum visitors, in their eyes, was not so much a representation of the crime as it was an extension of it.

Figure 2.3 Jewish women and children from Mizocz, German-occupied Poland, lined up by the SS moments before they were shot, October 14, 1942.

Photo: Naked Jewish women, some of whom are holding infants, wait in a line before their execution by German Sipo and SD, with the assistance of Ukrainian auxiliaries. United States Holocaust Memorial Museum Photo Archives # 17877. Courtesy of Instytut Pamieci Narodowej. Copyright of Instytut Pamieci Narodowej.

At the same time, despite the curators' stated aim of maintaining the exhibit's historical integrity, the museum may have refused to acknowledge another historical reality: the possibility of their visitors' prurient gaze. Will we ever know all the reasons why these images transfix people? Is the historical record of past travesties enough to close our eyes to the possibility of present travesties on the part of viewers? Can we say with certainty that every museum visitor's gaze is as pure as the curators' historical intent? The fine line between exhibition and exhibitionistic remains as fragile as it is necessary, even in the hands of conscientious historians and curators.

Where is the line between historical documentation of degradation and the re-degradation of victims? Can curators actually vouch for the integrity of every museum visitor's gaze? Almost from the first showing of photographs from the concentration camps, artists have attempted to plumb this question – or at least to ask it. Perhaps the earliest and most notorious were the survivor Boris Lurie's inflammatory installations and collages immediately after the war, including "Flatcar Assemblage by Adolf Hitler" (1945) and this work's elaboration in "Railroad Collage" (1959) and "Saturation Painting BUCHENWALD" (1959). In these works, the artist juxtaposed Margaret Bourke-White's iconic images of emaciated death camp survivors and piles of corpses stacked on a flatcar with other images of nudie pin-ups of the day. Here, he suggests, at least on the surface, that it is all pornography – but in so doing, he forces viewers to reevaluate their reasons for looking at such images altogether. As Norman Kleeblatt has noted, Lurie forces viewers to confront their own "voyeurism," which I take as their desire to regard the pain of others without being so regarded, their need to keep their reasons for looking at such images to themselves.[22]

As Boris Lurie makes explicitly clear in his various manifestoes for "No! Art!", the line between our gaze and the commodification of such images is almost non-existent. Once produced and recirculated, these images become cultural commodities to be traded, valued, and paid for. The potential for turning the suffering of women – or anyone – into so much "art for sale" or so much capital or cultural currency is also part of the photographic act. Strangely, it seems to take a conflating of sexuality and violence to bring this home to many people – as Boris Lurie surely knew when he assembled collages of death camp images surrounded by girlie magazine nudes and pin-ups of the 1950s.[23]

A few years later, German artist Gerhard Richter similarly broached the question as to whether the popular dissemination of Holocaust images amounted to a new, respectable kind of pornography. In his installation, *ATLAS*, Richter juxtaposed photographs of naked, tangled corpses next to sexually explicit images of naked and tangled bodies copulating.[24] His aim was not to eroticize the death camp scenes so much as it was to force viewers to ask uncomfortable questions of themselves: where is the line between the historically inquiring and the erotically preoccupied gaze? Where is the line between historical exhibition and sensationalistic exhibitionism? In fact, here we might even step back to ask whether any exhibition, even the most rigorously framed, can ever merely show such sensationalist imagery without descending into sensationalism. Can the artists, curators, or even we, as viewers, objectively critique such sensationalist images without participating in the sensation itself?

Is it also possible that insofar as Holocaust-era prisoners are regarded as powerless, humiliated, and dehumanized, they are also, on some level, regarded emblematically as women? To the extent that Jews as victims are often

[22] See Norman L. Kleeblatt, "The Nazi Occupation of the White Cube: Transgressive Images/Moral Ambiguity/Contemporary Art," in Norman L. Kleeblatt, Ed. *Mirroring Evil: Nazi Imagery/Recent Art* (New Brunswick and London: Rutgers University Press, 2002), an exhibition catalogue for "Mirroring Evil," a show at the Jewish Museum in New York City, 17 March – 30 June 2002, pp. 10-11.

[23] For more on Boris Lurie's work, see David Katz, "The Artist as Provocateur," *Jewish Quarterly* (October 2005); see also the artist's own website, www.NO!art.com.

[24] For a reproduction of this installation, see Gerhard Richter, *Atlas* (New York and London: Marian Goodman and Anthony D'Offay, 1997), pp. 16-23.

represented universally in the figure of the woman or the child (I would argue that to some extent, all pre-pubescent children are regarded as feminine, as more female than male, even the little boy in the Warsaw Ghetto with his arms upraised, in his knee-socks and short tunic (Figure 2.4), the victim is regarded as classically feminine. When this is so, however, little room is left in the story for women as women.

Figure 2.4 Boy with hand raised in the Warsaw Ghetto.

Photo: Jews captured by SS and SD troops during the suppression of the Warsaw ghetto uprising are forced to leave their shelter and march to the Umschlagplatz for deportation. United States Holocaust Memorial Museum Photo Archives # 26543. Courtesy of National Archives and Records Administration, College Park.

Sara Horowitz has argued persuasively that in many male Holocaust narratives, "women are presented as helpless (although the men were no less helpless), as absent loved ones (although the men, too, were absent), and as needing rescue (although the men, too needed rescue)."[25] Though Horowitz stops here with the fact of such representations, I believe she also hints at why men may have represented women in this way without saying so explicitly. Because men have been constitutively unable to speak of their helplessness, of their absence as loved ones, of their need to be rescued, of their inability to fulfill their masculine need to protect family, perhaps they have displaced their unspeakable condition onto their iconic representations of women as emblematic of all these conditions.

Moreover, I believe that many of these male writers' constitutive inability to see their oppression of women results in a parallel inability to see, or even to regard, the sexual abuse of Jewish women by the Nazis, thereby splitting off women's sexual violation during the Holocaust from their master-narrative of events. Or as Irene Eber once told Joan Ringelheim, "Male memory can confront women as victims, but cannot confront male oppression." That is, there seems

---

[25] Sara R. Horowitz, "Women in Holocaust Literature: Engendering Trauma Memory," in Ofer and Weitzman, Eds. *Women and the Holocaust,* p. 368.

to be neither language nor conceptual frame for articulating one's oppression of the other sex. Conversely, according to Irene Eber, "The same may be true for women survivors. They can see themselves as Nazi victims, but not as victims of Jewish men or even Nazi men, except perhaps as non-female victims. "

Similarly, it may also be difficult for women to describe their female oppressors without figuring them as masculine. I think here of Sarah Nomberg-Przytyk's depiction of the female Kapos in her barracks, the *stubowe*, who "in most instances were vulgar and coarse... [who] marched with a mannish step, their arms swinging at their sides."[26] Literally, both men and women have difficulty "regarding" the pain of women, except insofar as it is inflicted by the Nazis or by "mannish" women, and I would add, except when the women are portrayed as victims-ideal. That is, again, there may be no place in traditional governing paradigms for sexual victimization, certainly not in male memory – but not even perhaps in female memory.

Why the sexual and gender-specific atrocities of the Holocaust should be split off from our so-called master narratives of the Nazi genocide when such experiences have long found expression in the antecedent literature of destruction (such as the Biblical book of Lamentations and early twentieth-century pogrom poetry) is still not completely clear to me. In Lamentations, for example, a destroyed and vanquished Jerusalem is figured as a weeping woman whose "sanctuaries have been entered and treasures looted," whose children and husbands have been taken from her, but who is also to blame for her plight by her wanton behavior (in the tradition of *mipnei hata'enu*, or because of our sins).[27] So even as we have the ultimate destruction in Jewish tradition represented in the archetype of the suffering woman, the figure itself includes at least a reference to sexual violation as part of its internal logic.

Even more striking are the brutally raw depictions of sexual violation in Chaim Nachman Bialik's widely circulated, iconic 1903 Kishinev pogrom poem, "Ba'ir ha'regah" ("In the City of the Killing "), in which the men-folk are depicted as watching helplessly and voyeuristically while their wives, daughters, and mothers are raped and murdered by marauding Gentiles. Husbands, bridegrooms, and brothers hide in the shadows and, in the poet's language, are even perhaps titillated as they "peeped" (*hetzitzu min ha'chorim*) through the holes of their hiding places.

And behold, yea behold: In the darkness of that corner,

Beneath this matzah-trough and behind that cask,

---

[26] Sara Nomberg-Przytyk, *Auschwitz: True Tales from a Grotesque Land* (Chapel Hill and London: The University of North Carolina Press, 1985), p. 21.
[27] Lam. 1.8

Lay husbands, bridegrooms, brothers, peeping from the holes

While holy bodies quivered beneath asses' flesh,

Being strangled in their impurity and swallowing the blood of their throats

And like a man dividing his delicacies, so the abominable goy divides their flesh –

Lying down in their shame and seeing – neither stirring nor moving.[28]

Of course, Bialik's poem was also a call to arms in which he rejected all traditional responses to such attacks. Instead of rising to protect their women, the men only continued to "regard the pain of their women," which for Bialik amounted to a vicarious participation in the sexual violation of their women, even a substitute for preventing it. Part of the crime, in Bialik's radically subversive view here, was just this passive regard of women's suffering, which did not move them to question God's justice or to gouge their eyes out or go out of their minds, but only to pray to God for a miracle – "and not let such evil come upon me." Another part of the crime was the men's traditional religious response to the suffering of their women. Finally, when it was safe to come out, the husbands "burst forth from their holes" and rushed not to their women's aid but straight to their rabbis with the question, "Rabbi, my wife, what is she? Permitted or forbidden?"[29] That is, now that our wives have been raped, are they still sexually available to us?

Kishinev is attacked as a Jewish shtetl, Jewish women of the town are raped as women, and Jewish men "regard" the pain of Jewish women through the prism of Halacha (Jewish law). Thirty-eight years later, a Jewish girl in Warsaw goes into hiding as a Jew but is abused as a woman by non-Jews who are hiding her from the Nazis. The girl asks years later whether her experience as a Jew was thus to include her experiences as a woman, whether her experience of sexual abuse counted as part of her Holocaust story. The answer is that one experience is necessarily part of the other, and to split one from the other is to disintegrate this Jewish woman's experience during the Holocaust.

In Bialik's integrated view, the sexual violation of women during pogroms and the men's response to it were part and parcel of the pogrom. Part of the terror of pogroms was the absolute sexual violence against women, and here is Bialik in 1903, facing explicitly both the gendered responses of men and women to this

---

[28] Hebrew original and translation are from Steven L. Jacobs, *Shirot Bialik: A New and Annotated Translation of Chaim Nachman Bialik's Epic Poems* (Columbus: Alpha Publishing Company, 1987), pp. 134-136.
[29] Ibid., 136.

terror and the implications in our regard of it – at the moment and afterward. Remember how in Chaim Kaplan's diary, Kaplan asked plaintively at one point, referring to Bialik, "Oh poet of the people, where are you now?" For a long time after the Holocaust, poets like Bialik were hard to come by.

The proximity of death and sex, as explored in the arts of Holocaust memory, has mostly scandalized readers after World War II in ways that Bialik's inflammatory poem did not scandalize Jews in the Pale of Settlement. In fact, images of rape and bayoneted pregnant women stuffed with feather bedding by the killers were rife in pogrom poetry and theatre. Why, then, has there been so little place for sexual violation in Holocaust literature and poetry? Why have historians and critics so often assumed[30] that it is the sensationalizing media that has sexualized the Holocaust, as if sexual experience in the Holocaust was only rare and incidental and not somehow intrinsic to the suffering of so many women in the camps and ghettos? Ringelheim notes accurately I think that, for some reason, we can make mass rape an integral part of the genocide of Bosnian Muslims by Serbs in the 1990s. And as I've suggested, Bialik depicted rape as integral to the Kishinev pogrom. Why are the explicitly gendered and sexual experiences of women during the Holocaust only now being made part of its history and memory?

"Their secret was death, not sex." So begins Ruth Kluger's powerfully clear-eyed memoir, *Weiter Leben*, what she calls "A Holocaust Girlhood Remembered."[31] Kluger refers here to the "forbidden news" she strained to overhear as a child eavesdropping on her parents' salon in the days after her hometown Vienna's annexation by the Nazis. These horror stories were fascinating – even titillating for their opaqueness and what she called their "whiff of fantasy." Unlike most male survivor accounts and nearly all female survivors' remembrances, Kluger opens her remembrance by associating death and sex, not because they intrinsically belong together but because they were both unspeakable secrets. What sets Kluger's memoir apart from the others is her relentless integration of the unspeakable into life, into her attempts at "going on living." Whether it's anger at her mother and father or love for her German friends – it all gets spoken, leaving none of it fixed. Her story, unlike so many others, leaves room for all other stories, all of which go on living in hers.

Bibliography

Bataille, Georges. *Eroticism*. London: J. Calder, 1962.

Gutterman, Ella, and Avner Shalev, eds. *To Bear Witness: Holocaust Remembrance at Yad Vashem*. Jerusalem: Yad Vashem Publications, 2005.

---

[30] As Joan Ringelheim relates in "The Split between Gender and the Holocaust," in Ofer and Weitzman, Eds. *Women in the Holocaust*, p. 340.

[31] Ruth Kluger, *Still Alive: A Holocaust Girlhood Remembered* (New York: The Feminist Press of the City University of New York, 2001), p. 15.

Horowitz, Sara R. "Women in Holocaust Literature: Engendering Trauma Memory." In *Women and the Holocaust,* edited by Ofer and Weitzman, 364–77. New Haven, CT: Yale University Press, 1998.

Jacobs, Steven L. *Shirot Bialik: A New and Annotated Translation of Chaim Nachman Bialik's Epic Poems.* Columbus, OH: Alpha Publishing Company, 1987.

Kleeblatt, Norman L. "The Nazi Occupation of the White Cube: Transgressive Images / Moral Ambiguity / Contemporary Art." *Mirroring Evil: Nazi Imagery/Recent Art.* New York and New Brunswick, NJ: Jewish Museum and Rutgers University Press, 2001. Published in conjunction with the exhibition at the Jewish Museum, New York.

Kluger, Ruth. *Still Alive: A Holocaust Girlhood Remembered.* New York: Feminist Press of the City University of New York, 2001.

Levinthal, David. *Untitled [Women being shot].* 1994. Dye diffusion transfer print, 61.6 cm x 50 cm (24.25 in x 19.6875 in). Museum of Fine Arts Houston, Houston, TX. https://emuseum.mfah.org/objects/42118/untitled-women-being-shot.

Miller, Nancy K. "Cartoons of the Self: Portrait of the Artist as a Young Murderer—Art Spiegelman's *Maus.*" *M/e/a/n/i/n/g* 12 (November 1992): 43–54.

Nomberg-Przytyk, Sara. *Auschwitz: True Tales from a Grotesque Land.* Translated by Roslyn Hirsch. Chapel Hill: University of North Carolina Press, 1985.

Ringelheim, Joan. "The Split between Gender and the Holocaust." In *Women in the Holocaust,* edited by Ofer and Weitzman, 340–50. New Haven, CT: Yale University Press, 1998.

Smith, Bradley F., and Agnes F. Peterson, eds. *Heinrich Himmler: Geheimreden, 1933 bis 1945.* Frankfurt: Propylaen, 1974.

Sontag, Susan. *Regarding the Pain of Others.* New York: Farrar, Straus and Giroux, 2003.

——. *On Photography.* New York: Farrar, Straus and Giroux, 1973.

Spiegelman, Art. *Maus: A Survivor's Tale.* Volumes 1 and 2. New York: Pantheon, 1986, 1991.

Further Reading

Bronfen, Elisabeth. *Over Her Dead Body: Death, Femininity, and the Aesthetic.* New York: Routledge Press, 1992.

Fuchs, Esther, ed. *Women and the Holocaust: Narrative and Representation.* Lanham, MD: University Press of America, 1999.

Goldenberg, Myrna, and E. Baer, eds. *Experience and Expression: Women and the Holocaust.* Detroit: Wayne State University Press, 2003.

Heinemann, Marlene E. *Gender and Destiny: Women Writers and the Holocaust.* New York: Greenwood Press, 1986.

Horowitz, Sara R. "Gender, Genocide, and Jewish Memory." *Prooftexts* 20, no. 1–2 (2000): 158–90. https://www.jstor.org/stable/10.2979/prooftexts.20.1-2.0158.

Katz, David. "The Artist as Provocateur." *Jewish Quarterly* 52.3 (2005): 21–26.

Katz, Esther, and Joan Ringelheim, eds. *Proceedings of the Conference on Women Surviving: The Holocaust.* New York: Institute for Research in History, 1983.

Ofer, Dalia, and Lenore J. Weitzman, eds. *Women in the Holocaust.* New Haven, CT: Yale University Press, 1998.

Peskowitz, Miriam, and Laura Levitt, eds. *Judaism since Gender.* New York: Routledge, 1997.

Richter, Gerhard. *Atlas.* New York and London: Marian Goodman and Anthony D'Offay / Thames and Hudson Ltd., 1997.

Rittner, Carol, and John K. Roth, eds. *Different Voices: Women and the Holocaust.* New York: Paragon House, 1993.

Chapter 3

Refuge in the Imaginary: War Trauma and the Limits of Language in Ghada Samman's *Kawābīs Beirut* and Samar Yazbek's *Planet of Clay*

Layla AlAmmar

American University of Kuwait (AUK)

Abstract

This chapter argues that the female protagonists of Ghada Samman's *Kawābīs Beirut* and Samar Yazbek's *Planet of Clay* react to the utter breakdown of their social realities by retreating into the fantasy-laden, visual field of the Imaginary. Both protagonists write their stories under conditions of escalating violence as the Lebanese Civil War and the Syrian Civil War, respectively, erupt around them. Consequently, they reveal axiomatic aesthetics of trauma, such as compulsive repetitions and silence, which revert to Freudian understandings of trauma. However, by drawing on Jacques Lacan's register of orders, the analysis shifts from an individual, pathologizing view of the protagonists to the wider psychosocial implications of how the respective wars have ruptured the Symbolic and revealed the traumatic Real through neopatriarchal hegemonic structures. As the Symbolic is a language-mediated order of signifiers, the protagonists display anxieties regarding language's referential capacity to convey traumatic experiences. In both narratives, a semiotic, pre-symbolic dimension allows the protagonists to articulate trauma in a way that eschews the violent discourse of men.

Keywords*:* Symbolic and Imaginary, traumatic Real, Arab war literature, literary trauma theory, neopatriarchy

* * *

Since the mid-2000s, scholars have called for "de-colonizing" literary trauma theory, with the aim of expanding the field beyond its Euro-American roots, set down a decade earlier by Cathy Caruth and her peers in the Yale School. Subsequent efforts have focused on widening the scope of literary trauma to include non-Western histories, such as the legacies of slavery and the Middle Passage, as well as ongoing systems of racial oppression.[1] Much work has gone towards interrogating the limits of empathy, cross-cultural solidarity, and articulations of postcolonial grief.[2] Important interventions have expanded the parameters of literary trauma, its aesthetic modes of representation, as well as underlying psychoanalytic assumptions of subject formation.[3] However, with few exceptions, Arab literature has not been critically analyzed through the lenses provided by this rich field of study.

Initially, I found this neglect surprising given that it is almost too easy to map Caruthian literary trauma theory onto Arab narratives. Arab literature articulates moments of sociopolitical upheaval, which inevitably produce an array of trauma with which to contend. Whether it be anti-colonial independence movements, sectarian conflict, or ongoing oppression under authoritarian regimes, Arab fiction expresses trauma experienced by individuals and communities under conditions of violence. In addition, scholars have shown how this literature, particularly that of Arab women, often illuminates the impact of large-scale political trauma on the domestic sphere and normative gender relations.[4] Thus, the nature of trauma in these narratives is a complex interweaving of personal and political, individual and collective, insidious and overt, making it fruitful for exploration under the paradigm of literary trauma theory.

Moreover, Arab literature frequently deploys narrative styles that accord with an understanding of literary trauma as formulated by Caruth. Her theory was

---

[1] See Stef Craps and Gert Buelen, "Introduction: Postcolonial Trauma Novels," *Studies in the Novel* 40 (2008): 1-12; Stef Craps, *Postcolonial Witnessing: Trauma out of Bounds* (London: Palgrave Macmillan, 2013); and Abigail Ward, *Postcolonial Traumas: Memory, Narrative, Resistance* (London: Palgrave Macmillan, 2015).

[2] See David Eng and David Kazanjian, *Loss: The Politics of Mourning* (University of California Press, 2002); Paul Gilroy, *Postcolonial Melancholia* (New York: Columbia University Press, 2004); Sam Durrant, *Postcolonial Narrative and the Work of Mourning: J. M. Coetzee, Wilson Harris, and Toni Morrison* (State University of New York Press, 2004); and Hamish Dalley, "The Question of 'Solidarity' in Postcolonial Trauma Fiction: Beyond the Recognition Principle," *Humanities* 4, no. 3 (2015): 369-392.

[3] See Ranjana Khanna, *Dark Continents: Psychoanalysis and Colonialism* (Duke University Press, 2003); Claire Stocks, "Trauma Theory and the Singular Self: Rethinking Extreme Experiences in the Light of Cross Cultural Identity," *Textual Practice* 21, no. 1 (2007): 71–92; and Michelle Balaev, *Contemporary Approaches in Literary Trauma Theory* (London: Palgrave Macmillan, 2014).

[4] See Evelyne Accad, *Sexuality and War: Literary Masks of the Middle East* (New York University Press, 1990); Miriam Cooke, *War's Other Voices: Women Writers on the Lebanese Civil War* (Cambridge University Press, 1987); Anastasia Valassopoulos, *Contemporary Arab Women Writers: Cultural Expression in Context* (Routledge, 2007); and Lindsey Moore, *Narrating Postcolonial Arab Nations: Egypt, Algeria, Lebanon, Palestine* (Routledge, 2017).

entirely predicated on early Freudian psychoanalytic understandings of trauma and its impacts. The two main phenomena she borrows are repression and belatedness, which originate in Freud's *Studies on Hysteria*.[5] Thus, silence and unspeakability serve as evidence of the inaccessibility of the trauma, with narratives and characters within them circling a core memory that they cannot adequately grasp, or *claim*, as Caruth would say. She argues that "the impact of the traumatic event lies precisely in its belatedness, in its refusal to be simply located, in its insistent appearance outside the boundaries of any single place or time."

For this reason, she asserts that trauma narratives display non-linear chronologies where temporal disjunction abounds, and the past violently erupts into the present. According to Caruth, "to be traumatized is precisely to be possessed by an image or an event,"[6] which was not psychically assimilated when it occurred. Consequently, the effects of this exceptional occurrence manifest in debilitating symptoms, such as hallucinations and flashbacks, rendering trauma "a repeated suffering of the event."[7]

And yet, despite such axiomatic markers of literary trauma theory being evident across Arab literature, this body of work has been neglected by the field, both in its initial formulations as well as following calls to "decolonize." I would argue the reasons for this neglect are analogous to, if not symptomatic of, the neglect of the Middle East within the wider field of postcolonial studies. Anna Ball and Karim Mattar assert that "postcolonial studies were [...] articulated as a field whose central concern was the anglophone and francophone literature of (former) colonies in South Asia, Africa, the Caribbean, and Oceania, and by migrants from these regions to the (former) imperial metropolis."[8] This framework leaves many Arab contexts in ambiguous positions, from Palestinian anti-colonialist struggles to democratic movements against totalitarian oppression in Syria to sectarian conflicts in Lebanon, which cannot be reduced to and centered on colonial experiences. Furthermore, the region's contexts are considered too varied, its politics too strained, and the Arabic language too

---

[5] This theory of trauma is two-stage: Stage I is the first forgotten impact, which is not assimilated as it occurs and is repressed; Stage II is the belated return of the event, or *nachträglichkeit* ("belatedness"), signaled by distressing psychosomatic symptoms. For more, see Sigmund Freud and Joseph Breuer. *The standard edition of the complete psychological works of Sigmund Freud. Vol. 2 (1893-1895): Studies on Hysteria*. The Hogarth Press & The Institute of Psychoanalysis, 1957, pp. 1-17.

[6] Ibid., 5.

[7] Ibid., 10.

[8] Ball, Anna & Karim Mattar. "Dialectics of Post/Colonial Modernity in the Middle East: A Critical, Theoretical and Disciplinary Overview." *The Edinburgh Companion to the Postcolonial Middle East* (Edinburgh University Press, 2019), 4.

demanding to allow for integration into the existing parameters of postcolonial studies.[9] In addition, literary trauma theory initially conceived of the traumatized person as a member of a dominant group, such as US veterans of the Vietnam War.[10] Arab literature on the 2003 invasion of Iraq, for instance, would not focus on the trauma of the American soldier but rather on the Iraqi people and the psychosocial effects of cyclical and compounded violence in their homeland. Moreover, "Western" actors may be absent from these narratives, with the conflict being of a sectarian nature or against totalitarian regimes. Consequently, the few scholars who have approached Arab literature through this lens have a personal link to the region and have largely limited themselves to the application of literary trauma theory without necessarily repudiating the field's core formulations.[11]

I contend that reading Arab fiction, particularly that of women, illuminates the central problem of a Freudian contemplation of trauma, where the experience is viewed as an exceptional event that has been thrust into some inaccessible dark corner of the mind, left to produce distressing effects. Arab literature overturns this very basic assumption to show that there are places in the world where trauma is not exceptional nor bound by the spatiotemporal framework through which events are defined. On the contrary, there are contexts where trauma is recurring, quotidian, and inherited. The historical circumstances underlying the two texts explored in this chapter – the Lebanese Civil War (1975-1990) and the Syrian Civil War (2011-present) – defy nearly all the foundational characteristics of literary trauma theory. Ghada Samman's *Kawābīs Beirut* (1976, translated as *Beirut Nightmares* in 1997) and Samar Yazbek's *Planet of Clay* (2021) both take place under states of siege. In the former, the unnamed female protagonist cannot leave her apartment as what became known as the "Battle of the Hotels" erupts in her neighborhood in central Beirut, while in the latter, fourteen-year-old Rima narrates her story in the summer of 2013 during the siege of Eastern Ghouta.[12] Both protagonists write their stories while trapped in locations with dwindling resources and under the unabating sounds of war. They witness and

[9] See Waïl S. Hassan, "Postcolonialism and Modern Arabic Literature: Twenty-first-century Horizons." *The Edinburgh Companion to the Postcolonial Middle East* (Edinburgh University Press, 2019, pp. 43-56).

[10] See Roger Luckhurst, *The Trauma Question* (Routledge, 2008).

[11] See Hanadi Al-Samman, *Anxiety of Erasure: Trauma, Authorship, and the Diaspora in Arab Women's Writings* (Syracuse University Press, 2015).

[12] The "Battle of the Hotels", a sub-conflict of the war, began in October 1975 and took place in Beirut's hotel district. Militias exchanged heavy rounds of rocket and gunfire, and snipers were used extensively. Different factions vied for the tactically valuable vantage points which the hotels would allow them to occupy, and the Holiday Inn (featured in Samman's novel) was a prime target. For more see Edgar O'Ballance. *Civil War in Lebanon, 1975-1992* (London: Palgrave Macmillan, 1998).

are subject to horrifying violence, including shootings, bombings, the murder of loved ones, chemical attacks, and the accumulation of corpses in their immediate surroundings. These are settings the likes of which Freud could never have conceived and which, thus, fundamentally challenge Caruthian formulations of literary trauma.

In this chapter, I go beyond Freud, drawing on Jacques Lacan's tripartite register of orders to argue that both protagonists revert to the fantasy-laden, visual field of the Imaginary to cope with the breakdown of the Symbolic order surrounding them. In fact, war ruptures the Symbolic and reveals the traumatic Real at its core, which I contend manifests as neopatriarchal hegemonic structures that continually generate war paradigms. As the Symbolic is a language-mediated order governed by signifiers, the protagonists display anxieties regarding the adequacy of language in conveying their traumatic experiences. However, despite finding some refuge in the Imaginary, both are ultimately made to confront the Symbolic. I argue that Samman's protagonist, who, as a writer, was predisposed towards the tools of the Symbolic, eventually accedes to the logic of the war. At the same time, Rima's narrative ends with her alone and abandoned without having submitted to the hegemonic neopatriarchal order.

In what follows, I am by no means advocating a wholesale rejection of Freudian psychoanalysis in the study of Arab women's literature. I believe Freud's studies of the hysteric, mourning melancholia, the ego, and the critical agency of the superego can prove invaluable in illuminating the ways in which human beings attempt to move through their worlds. However, Lacan's structure of orders and their *material* implications provide a rich space for theorizing the manner in which Arab women writers contest the hegemonic neopatriarchal societies that characterize much of the modern Arabic-speaking world and which, I believe, lie at the core of recurring cycles of sociopolitical conflict and large-scale trauma.[13]

War Ruptures the Symbolic and Reveals the Traumatic Real

Kawābīs Beirut and *Planet of Clay* document the early phases of what would become atrociously violent and protracted civil wars. The former takes place

---

[13] Hisham Sharabi defines neopatriarchy as "the outcome of modern Europe's colonization of the patriarchal Arab world" (21). It is predicated on a unique form of patriarchy that arose in traditional Arab society, which encompasses a "specific psychosociological totality" that did not undergo the necessary transformation during the *nahda* (nineteenth century Arab Awakening). Neopatriarchal societies are characterized by a "fetishized modernism," where "ideas, actions, values, or institutions are validated (or invalidated) not by criticism but by reference to a model" (24). Thus, modernity across the Arabic-speaking world largely represents "material modernization, the first (surface) manifestation of social change," which "only served to remodel and reorganize patriarchal structures and relations and to reinforce them by giving them "modern" forms and appearances" (4). For more, see Hisham Sharabi, *Neopatriarchy: A Theory of Distorted Change in Arab Society* (Oxford University Press, 1992).

over two weeks in the first year of the Lebanese Civil War, which would last fifteen years. The latter takes place during the summer of 2013, a little over a year into the Syrian Civil War, which continues to the present day. Both protagonists choose to articulate their experiences in writing. In Samman's novel, the protagonist is a writer and translator for "a revolutionary publishing house."[14] So her instinct is to begin immediately documenting the occurrences around her in a series of episodes she calls "Nightmares."[15] In Yazbek's narrative, Rima is a teenager with selective mutism who struggles to "form relationships between words and real life."[16] As such, both novels attempt to convey the rupture that sudden large-scale violence enacts in the Symbolic order and which upsets its presumed stability.

"Don't think that what you are reading is a novel," Rima states at the start of the narrative, "what I'm writing is the truth, and I am doing it to try and understand what happened."[17] With this statement, she reveals core anxieties displayed throughout the story, which revolve around the referential capacity of language in representing material trauma, the relationship between words and their meanings, as well as her ability to maintain authorial control amidst the chaos around her. Rima lives on the outskirts of Damascus with her mother and brother, where they attempt to survive the violence of the Syrian Civil War. One of the first things the reader learns about Rima is she has a condition that distinguishes her in two main ways. Firstly, she has a compulsion to walk, so her mother ties their wrists together when they venture outside. Secondly, Rima refuses to speak. Throughout the novel, she stresses that her silence is voluntary, despite what people assume: "I wasn't mute; I could recite the Qur'an, but I have no wish to speak."[18] And though her condition pre-dates the war, the trauma to which she is exposed results in an obsessive concern with words as well as heightened anxiety surrounding narrative control as she writes to a reader she self-consciously addresses. In describing her, Yazbek notes, "Rima embodies a number of themes [...], such as women's freedom, the relationship between writing and violence, and the new language we might construct in the midst of the terrible events we are living through."[19] The war has fractured the Symbolic order, leading to uncertainty regarding the referential capacity of language to represent traumatic experiences.

---

[14] Ghada Samman, *Kawābīs Beirut* (11th ed., *Manshurat Ghada al-Samman*, 2020), 41.
[15] I quote my translation of the Arabic rather than the published English translation as many key episodes were omitted.
[16] Samar Yazbek, *Planet of Clay*, trans. Leri Price (World Editions, 2021), 75.
[17] Ibid., 19.
[18] Ibid., 86.
[19] This statement appears on the inner fly-leaf of the first edition.

Rima's apprehension is not limited to whether words are adequate in assigning meaning but also whether the reader shares such meanings or, indeed, if they can be *conveyed* to the reader at all. Early in the narrative, when she and her mother are traveling through variously-held territories to visit Rima's teacher, Sitt Souad, she states, "No doubt you know what a checkpoint is and there is no need for me to explain it to you, although the relationship between a word and its meaning occupies me a lot."[20] When her mother is shot and killed while trying to protect her, Rima begins using the word "disappeared" to describe loved ones who are killed in order to distance herself from the trauma of their deaths.

For Samman's protagonist, the situation is more complex. As a well-known writer who pens a weekly column for a magazine, she is aware of her active role in fashioning the apparatus that has resulted in war. She employs the tools of the Symbolic order, language, and signifiers in order to express herself and communicate sociopolitical convictions she shares with other intellectuals. Consequently, the violent manifestations of her articulations, with snipers shooting everything that moves and corpses accumulating in front of her apartment building, haunt her throughout the narrative. She compulsively reiterates feelings of culpability at how the tools of the Symbolic order have resulted in such carnage: "These were my letters. They had emerged from inside the books to become human beings, bearing arms and killing."[21]

In the 1950s, Lacan framed the Symbolic order as a dimension of language that structures the individual's unconscious and thus becomes a determinant of subjectivity: "The unconscious is the sum of the effects of speech on a subject, at the level at which the subject constitutes himself out of the effects of the signifier."[22] As Lacan conceived of language as constituting subjectivity, he came to view subjectivity itself, Celia Britton states, "as a question of structural relations and transformations rather than a substantive entity."[23] The Symbolic order is then defined as "the pre-existing transindividual matrix of signification on which man is fundamentally dependent. [It] governs all forms of social organization [...] and intervenes as a mediating third term in all relations between individuals."[24] Returning to Freud's Oedipus Complex, Lacan saw the figure of the father as representing the Other, the wider world of Law and signifiers that pre-date and constitute the subject – "we depend on the field of

---

[20] Ibid., 26.

[21] Samman, 41.

[22] Jacques Lacan, *The Four Fundamental Concepts of Psycho-Analysis*, trans. Alan Sheridan (Penguin, 1994), 126.

[23] Celia Britton. "Structuralist and Poststructuralist Psychoanalytic and Marxist Theories." *The Cambridge History of Literary Criticism* (Cambridge University Press, 1995, pp. 197-252), 198.

[24] Ibid., 202.

the Other, which was there long before we came into the world, and whose circulating structures determine us as subjects. "[25] Thus, the child's identification with (and submission to) the *name of the father* is where their social reality is mediated to them and marks their entry into the Symbolic order.

Logic dictates that what Lacan calls the Symbolic order is, in fact, many Symbolic orders, and whichever order an individual is born into is the one that determines their subjectivity. Britton emphasizes that Lacan's is "a *materialist* account of the subject, who, far from being an autonomous self-generating spirit, is produced by the material agency of the signifier – constituted *by* his insertion *into* the Symbolic order."[26] For the protagonists in *Kawābīs Beirut* and *Planet of Clay*, this order takes the form of neopatriarchal societies that continually generate war paradigms, leading to recurring cycles of trauma. Hisham Sharabi asserts that neopatriarchal societies are "highly unstable formation[s], riven by inner contradictions and conflicts."[27] Also governed by the rule of the father, these societies are characterized by a "generalized, persistent, and seemingly insurmountable impotence: [they are] incapable of performing as an integrated social or political system, as an economy, or as a military structure."[28] In both novels, the outbreak of war ruptures this order, and the protagonists register the breakdown by questioning the Symbolic order's language-mediated structure. Thus, both women interrogate the function of language and the integrity of signifiers and, ultimately, reject the structure and seek refuge in the Imaginary.

Both narrators display axiomatic responses to trauma, including silence, compulsive repetition, and somatic effects. For Samman's protagonist, whenever the sound of gunfire abates, her apartment falls into periods of what she calls "agitated, frightening, [...] unbelievably nightmarish silence."[29] She and her brother do not converse because "it was as though the sound of bullets had eliminated language."[30] In *Planet of Clay*, silence is also frightening and "weigh[s] heavily" on Rima because "silence brought painful things," often signaling the lull between the arrival of planes that drop bombs on the village.[31] Silence is an axiomatic response documented across literary trauma theory as it reverts to Freud's notion of trauma as inaccessible and, therefore, unspeakable. However, the subsequent challenging of this Eurocentrically-formed notion has spurred scholars to seek alternative theories for the persistent use of silence within

---

[25] Lacan, 126.
[26] Britton, 203.
[27] Sharabi, 4.
[28] Ibid., 7.
[29] Samman, 22.
[30] Ibid., 12.
[31] Yazbek, 156.

postcolonial narratives. To that end, it has been posited as a legitimate coping mechanism.[32] In terms of Arab literature, silences in Syrian narratives have been linked to the chronic trauma of living under an oppressive state apparatus where the precarity of daily life necessitates inventive modes of expressing traumatic histories, including surrealist and absurdist storytelling.[33]

Samman and Yazbek's protagonists also display compulsive repetitions, which go hand-in-hand with repression and belatedness. The former engages in repetitions that are related to the senses of the body, primarily sight, as though she can no longer trust these faculties. In fact, in Nightmare 32, she notes that "when life becomes a nightmare, the senses become instruments of torture."[34] Repetitions are pronounced throughout the narrative, such as in Nightmare 14, where she relays a hallucinatory account wherein, she claims to have witnessed a man poisoning the city's water supply with a "madness powder." In the account, which is only a paragraph long, she repeats the phrase "I watched" eleven times before ending with the statement, "I don't know if I was asleep or not... If I drank from the water or not."[35] In *Planet of Clay*, Rima also engages in compulsive repetitions centering on the accuracy of her memory as well as her ability to articulate a comprehensive narrative. She oscillates between using storytelling as a way to prompt remembrance – "I wouldn't have remembered what happened if I wasn't trying to explain the story to you" – while at other times, she acknowledges that the trauma of her mother's death has fundamentally altered the functions of her mind: "I can't remember for you how those two years passed. What happened at the checkpoint has made me lose my memories."[36] Her traumatic repetitions also assume the form of continuous assertions that she remains in control of the story – "Sitt Souad is another story I will tell you. There are many stories you will hear if I live. The important thing now is that I tell you how my mother disappeared."[37]

Repetitions correspond to Freud's return of the repressed, with the traumatized person engaging in what Dominick LaCapra terms "acting-out" where "the past is performatively regenerated or relived as if it were fully present rather than represented in memory and inscription, and it hauntingly returns as the repressed." [38] However, repetitions, through engaged memory work, can also

---

[32] See Stef Craps, "Beyond Eurocentrism: Trauma Theory in the Global Age," *The Future of Trauma Theory: Contemporary Literary and Cultural Criticism* (Routledge, 2014, pp. 45-61).
[33] See Mohja Kahf, "The Silence of Contemporary Syrian Literature," *World Literature Today* (Issue 75, 2001, 224-236).
[34] Samman, 38.
[35] Ibid., 20.
[36] Yazbek, 39, 41.
[37] Ibid., 20.
[38] Dominick LaCapra, "Trauma, Absence, Loss." *Critical Inquiry* 25, no. 4 (1999): 715-716.

serve a cathartic function, leading to what he terms "working through, " which "should be understood as an open, self-questioning process that never attains closure and counteracts acting-out without entirely transcending it, especially with respect to trauma and its aftermath."[39] Of course, these formulations are predicated on a trauma that occurred in the past, whereas the protagonists in *Kawābīs Beirut* and *Planet of Clay* recount trauma as it is being lived. Consequently, paradigmatic readings of repetition do not hold for these texts, and we may turn to Lacanian psychoanalysis for a more illuminating take. Nadia Bou Ali usefully illustrates how, with respect to language, "the repetition compulsion in literature [...] is the result of an encounter with the Real (opposed to the Symbolic and Imaginary)."[40] Building on Lacan's understanding of the unconscious, she argues that this aspect of the psyche, "which is the locus of the repetition compulsion and the site of the return of the repressed," gestures to what is fundamentally inconsistent in the objective world.[41] Thus, we can understand the protagonists' repetitions not as a re-staging of past trauma but as indications that a rupture in the Symbolic has revealed the traumatic Real at its core.

In both novels, masculinist war paradigms are presented as the product of neopatriarchal societies, which are inherited by young boys and, consequently, become self-perpetuating. Both texts feature scenes where young boys carry sticks, which they pretend are rifles. Towards the end of the narrative, when Rima is trapped in a basement, she sees two boys passing by. She has difficulty describing them as they appeared as "two little men, not boys [...] they were moving lightly, their bodies moved like men, but they were just boys."[42] Rima notes that "the older boy carried a stick on his back, and he had tied it with a rope like a rifle, " which he later swung through the air "as the men do here with their guns" while making gunfire sounds.[43] In *Kawābīs Beirut,* the protagonist recounts an incident where young boys loot a local toy store. Every night, their leader, eleven-year-old Karim, watches his father return home drenched in blood, boasting of the people he has tortured and killed in the name of the sectarian conflict. Coming from a low-income family, Karim dreams of mountains of toys, and so, along with other boys in the neighborhood, he breaks into the local toy store. The boys ransack the place, tearing the heads off of dolls and amassing toy guns and tanks. Hearing the commotion in the street outside, they

[39] Dominick LaCapra, *History in Transit: Experience, Identity, Critical Theory* (Cornell University Press, 2004), 92.
[40] Nadia Bou Ali, *Psychoanalysis and the Love of Arabic: Hall of Mirrors* (Edinburgh University Press, 2020), 23.
[41] Ibid., 23.
[42] Yazbek, 292.
[43] Ibid., 292, 295.

try to escape, but one of the boys is impaled on the broken glass of the window they had crawled through to enter the store. The boys pull the body down, and then the scene devolves into a nightmare where the guns become real, and they begin shooting one another. The episode ends with the survivors returning home "bleeding but still clutching their weapons tightly."

Consequently, though young boys may initially see war games as harmless fantasies, as they mature, this can materialize into a violent social reality. Furthermore, this episode suggests that war games serve to desensitize young boys to the violence in which they may partake in the future. These scenes, across both novels, indicate that masculinist war paradigms are an inheritance built into the neopatriarchal hegemonic Symbolic order and passed down from father to son.

Refuge in the Imaginary

In the novels, male and female characters differ in their responses to the rupture that war introduces to the Symbolic order. Where the protagonists articulate the causes of manifold trauma and its effects, male characters respond by clinging more tightly to neopatriarchal hegemonies. In *Kawābīs Beirut*, the protagonist's neighbor, Amm Fu'ad, insists she spend her nights in the apartment he shares with his son for protection after her brother is arrested. Amm Fu'ad is a product of Sharabi's "marriage of imperialism and patriarchy"; Western-educated, he prefers speaking French, carts around an antique Arab sword, and is "determined to die surrounded by his antiques, his badges of honor, and his house of stone."[44] He and his son, Amin, carry on with their lives as though the war is not raging on their doorstep. They continue to practice "proper etiquette" when the protagonist is a guest in their home, such as dinner being served by a cook in "a white jacket with gold buttons" on a table fully set with "golden spoons shining on the purple velvet tablecloth."[45] They also expect their house servant to continue performing his duties, such as risking exposure to snipers in order to feed Amin's pet monkey, which is kept in a cage on the roof of the apartment building. Where Amm Fu'ad and Amin's behavior elicits mockery in the protagonist – at the lavish dinner, she muses that "if one must starve, it ought to be 'according to proper etiquette'"[46] – the responses of male characters in *Planet of Clay* are fatally consequential.

After Rima's mother is killed, she and her brother flee in search of safety, ending up in a house with several families who are trying to escape the violence. However, the house does not provide sanctuary, as she reports that "in five days,

---

[44] Ibid., 21, 106.
[45] Ibid., 124.
[46] Ibid., 146.

we were bombed four times."[47] The final bomb falls on the house next door, and when Rima looks over to its courtyard, she sees "bits of bodies scattered all over" and that three of the women "had disappeared along with three children."[48] Later, she recounts the chemical attack on the neighborhood, into which her brother "disappears" and, subsequently, his friend Hassan is charged with her care. She testifies to the "bubbles with the horrible smell" and how he sprinkled water on her, wrapped her in a cover, and took off some of her chemical-soaked clothes.[49] Seeing this, a man shouts at him, saying, "*That's sinful, respect her hurma.*"[50] Hassan ignores him and continues washing Rima, who sees the bodies of dead women, still "wrapped in clothes with hijabs covering their heads." He later explains that the planes had dropped bombs containing poison gas and "these gases can penetrate clothing," so the person must be stripped immediately. However, as the men "said it was sinful for women to be uncovered in front of men," the women had been forced to stay clothed and so had died.[51] Rima later recounts seeing "a group of naked men, and on the opposite side, there was a group of women, fully dressed. The women were dead."[52] Consequently, even in times of extreme violence, some men are unwilling to relinquish atavistic male norms, even if it results in women's deaths.

The Symbolic order around them has broken down, and their response is to cling to strict masculinist paradigms, such as those embodied in *hurma* – a complex notion pertaining to confinement, tribal honor, and patriarchal control of women. The word itself translates to "inviolability," but given its unique cultural connotations, the text transliterates the term, and it remains un-glossed. I would argue that keeping the word in Arabic also gestures to the limits of language and its referential capacity to convey affective resonances. The notion of *hurma* is a uniquely Arab-Islamic one, difficult to convey in its totality to a reader unfamiliar with neopatriarchal Muslim-majority societies. *Hurma* is attributed to women – thus the man commanding Hassan to "respect her *hurma*" – but this "sanctity" belongs to her only inasmuch as she belongs to a man. Yaseen Noorani argues that their "usage to signify a woman or women derives not from any spatial idea, but from the *hurma*, the sanctity, and inviolability, of the women's relationship to the man in authority over them."[53] Here, Noorani discusses the

---

[47] Yazbek, 130.
[48] Ibid., 153-154.
[49] Ibid., 154.
[50] Ibid., 180.
[51] Ibid., 181.
[52] Ibid., 188.
[53] Yaseen Noorani, "Normative Notions of Public and Private in Early Islamic Culture," in *Harem Histories: envisioning places and living spaces*, ed. Marilyn Booth (Duke University Press, 2010), 53.

related terms *haram* (denoting sacred spaces, such as mosques), *harem,* and *harīm* (wives and/or womenfolk of men).

Furthermore, Noorani links this mastery of the male over his women to the wider social order where insofar as the "male individual achieves self-integration and thus social virtue through his mastery of a fiery interiority consisting of chaotic desire, so does the social order constitute itself through men's mastery and control of the women under their authority."[54] In other words, a man's mastery over his women indicates his self-mastery, which in turn gestures to the stability of the Symbolic order in which these subjectivities have been constituted. And so, to return to the narrative, what the man is actually saying is "respect that which belongs to another man." This becomes clear when Hassan, in order to appease him, claims Rima is his sister. Hearing this, the man is pacified and leaves them alone.

If male characters respond to ruptures in the Symbolic order by clinging to atavistic masculine paradigms, the reaction of female characters is to reject the Symbolic order and seek refuge in the fantasy-laden field of the Imaginary. The Imaginary is roughly analogous to Julia Kristeva's semiotic, pre-Oedipal space of the *chora* (Greek for enclosed space or womb), which emphasizes art, poetry, and myth as "irreducible to the 'language' object" and thus manifests as ruptures, deviations, and transgressions of language.[55]

Scholars have linked this poetic, imaginary sphere with Hélène Cixous's *écriture féminine* as a genre of writing distinct from masculine expression in its manner of articulating female difference (body, sexuality, cultural, and psychological) through language. In her discussion of Ghada Samman's short story collection, *The Square Moon,* Hanadi Al-Samman links the two – through Samman's use of surrealist, fantastical motifs – in order to argue for revolutionary potential, where a hegemonic, masculinist narrative is subverted by a collectivist, feminine one. She asserts that:

> The future can no longer depend solely on the language of the Father but should include the discourse of collective national voices, including that of the feminine. Fantasy genre becomes the vehicle for social critique and the mode that facilitates trauma recovery, reconciliation, and synthesis of conflicting histories and archives.[56]

In my view, reading the semiotic as inherently revolutionary misses a crucial point, which is that, like Lacan's Imaginary, the semiotic is ordered and mediated

---

[54] Ibid., 50.
[55] Julia Kristeva, *The Kristeva Reader* (London: Blackwell, 1986), 91.
[56] Hanadi Al-Samman, *Anxiety of Erasure: Trauma, Authorship, and the Diaspora in Arab Women's Writings* (Syracuse University Press, 2015), 133.

by the Symbolic. Consequently, an utterance in the *chora* remains subject to the Law. In other words, literature itself is constrained by "the fact that it signifies" and is articulated like a language. Thus, it is subject to the law of "the symbolic dimension which is given in language," and its articulation becomes "a specific expression of that law."[57] Consequently, the semiotic space of the *chora* is not as revolutionary as it first appears. As the two protagonists here illustrate, it is but a temporary refuge from a Symbolic order that has become unbearable.

In *Kawābīs Beirut,* the conceit of the novel takes place in a realm of fantasy, hallucinations, and surreal phantasmic occurrences. As mentioned previously, the text is not divided by chapters but by episodes numbered as Nightmares. In some, the protagonist documents her entrapment in the apartment, listening to battles raging outside. In contrast, others consist of flashbacks to life before the war with her lover, Yousef, who is killed at the start of the violence. Other nightmares, however, are pure hallucinations, imagined scenarios, and quasi-fables, which nevertheless convey the machinations that have led to war as well as their implications. For Rima, her retreat into the Imaginary consists of visual metaphors, such as bubbles, spheres, drawings, and colors. She also makes appeals to fantastical inter-texts, with allusions to *The Little Prince* and *Alice in Wonderland.* I contend that both protagonists turn to the Imaginary in response to the traumatic Real, which the breakdown of the Symbolic has uncovered. This retreat to the Imaginary is an attempt to cover the lack that the rupture of war has revealed.

According to Lacan, the subject is fundamentally and variously divided, first by their inauguration into the Imaginary through the Mirror Stage, followed by further division by language through insertion in the Symbolic order. He conceived of the Mirror Stage as a phase of human mental development where a child (between six to eighteen months of age) recognizes their reflection in a mirror. However, this recognition is, in fact, a *mis*-recognition (*méconnaissance*) in that the child perceives the image as a whole while they lack mastery over their body. This perceived discord between the wholeness of the image and the fragmentation of the body leads to an aggressive tension that the subject feels towards its image and, consequently, towards itself.[58] After that, the ego is formed from this self-alienating "drama [...] which manufactures for the subject, caught up in the lure of spatial identification, the succession of phantasies that extends from a fragmented body-image to a form of its totality."[59]

---

[57] Kristeva, 25.

[58] Jacques Lacan, "The Mirror Stage," in *Reading French Psychoanalysis,* ed. Dana Birksted-Breen, Sara Flanders, and Alain Gibeault (Routledge, 2010), 97-98.

[59] Ibid., 100.

However, there is another individual who is often present in this drama of psyche formation. The mother is usually the one holding the child up to the mirror, and she affirms their (mis)recognition by pointing at their reflection and saying, "Yes, that's you!" And so, the Imaginary order begins with this mother-child dyad; this is a sensory, affective state where, for the most part, language is unnecessary. Unable to speak, the infant vocalizes their desires in cries and whimpers, and the mother is able to recognize, decipher, and satisfy these desires. Kristeva's notion of the semiotic is useful in thinking about this quasi-undifferentiated realm as an emotional field where any linguistics consist of what Hanadi Al-Samman calls "free-floating, less-defined experiences of the self that seem to belong to the presymbolic world."[60] Al-Samman argues that female protagonists employ an "imaginary language" through which "dreams, telepathy, and sensory experience can replace the cold, repressive, and calculating male expressive modes."[61] Her larger argument is that by inhabiting this "liminal space," Arab women writers "shatter the whole male/female binary opposition paradigm," which ultimately "fosters healing and female empowerment" and halts the cycle of trauma.[62] However, it is unclear how (and indeed whether) this healing occurs, and there is no evidence that recurring cycles of political and personal trauma have been broken by such literary interventions. This is because these semiotic utterances remain subject to the Law, to the Symbolic, even as they attempt to transgress it.

Nevertheless, in *Kawābīs Beirut,* when bombs are exploding outside her apartment, the protagonist falls into a semi-conscious state, which she describes as a "sensory sphere that resides in every person though they've forgotten how to access it, [...] an astonishing sphere where one can grasp what lies beyond the everyday, familiar social reality."[63] And when she expresses in the same passage how this realm brings to mind the comfort of her "mother's womb," we can view it as a clear signal of her retreat into the *chora*, an order of the psyche that pre-dates the masculinist violence of the Symbolic order in which she finds herself. As for Rima, despite her voluntary silence, she asserts, "There is a gap in me that I have to speak about."[64] This gap is the traumatic Real that war has uncovered and which she attempts to articulate. Recognizing that the linguistic tools of the Symbolic are inadequate for "speaking" about this gap, she goes on to say that "it comes accompanied by pictures like drawings in water, and I understand events around me in this way... as drawings like water."[65] She claims

---

[60] Al-Samman, 120.

[61] Ibid., 124.

[62] Ibid., 124-125.

[63] Samman, 26.

[64] Yazbek, 185.

[65] Ibid., 185.

that "drawing was more capable of expression than words, and that lines and curves and corners and colors were more responsive," and thus, she relies on colors and shapes to convey meaning to the reader.[66] Consequently, following the chemical attack, she says, "I am trying to write the story of the bubbles by drawing letters. I will be optimistic and assume you will be able to solve this riddle of letters and drawings."[67]

As previously stated, both protagonists recognize the inherited nature of the masculinist war paradigms that govern their Symbolic orders – as evidenced by the scenes of young boys playing with pretend guns and emulating the destructive, violent behavior of adult men. In *Kawābīs Beirut,* the protagonist uses the Imaginary to argue that the cycle of trauma-perpetuating inheritance can be broken by smashing the Symbolic order itself. In Nightmare 47, she constructs an imaginary scene where a father gives his son gifts over a series of birthdays. On the first birthday, he presents him with a rifle, but the boy is disappointed, saying he wanted a bicycle with which he could "ride a rainbow and discover all of its colors."[68] On the second birthday, the father gives him a toy cannon, and the boy is again disappointed, saying he wants a paper plane with which he can fly with the birds. On the third birthday, he is given a gun which, when fired, his father says "will sound like exploding bombs." Again, the boy is dismayed, saying he would have preferred a guitar. On the fourth birthday, the father gives him a grenade, which he says is powerful enough "to kill an entire tribe." The boy perks up and removes the clip, tossing the grenade towards his parents, killing them and causing the house to collapse. The protagonist notes that "the neighbors do not ask what happened [...] for the same event had been occurring in nearly every house."[69] This is not quite Freud's killing of the primal father by a band of brothers, the guilt from which ultimately inaugurates religion and a move away from the "horde mentality" toward civilization.[70] However, there is some relevance to be found in his late work. Drawing on Freud's final text, *Moses and Monotheism,* Bou Ali argues that for Freud, "the paternal law, or the name-of-the-father" (the Symbolic order) is one where the social bond is supported "through some form of murderous betrayal" and is therefore "plagued and haunted by transgressions, transmitted in myth, culture, ritual, etc."[71] In other words, violence is built into and

---

[66] Ibid., 200.
[67] Ibid., 167.
[68] Samman, 56.
[69] Ibid., 56.
[70] Sigmund Freud. *Totem and taboo: Resemblances between the psychic lives of savages and neurotics* (Ktoczyta.pl, 2020), 110-113.
[71] Bou Ali, 66. The betrayal is the murder of Moses by a group of his followers, which has been psychically passed down the Jewish collective and has resulted in a group dynamic

sustained by this structure from its earliest, most primordial beginnings, and this violence is reenacted and transmitted in various ways throughout history. Consequently, Samman argues that mere resistance, through words or empty gestures, is insufficient; the entire structure must be obliterated, and a new psychosocial reality must be constructed in its place.

Though the Imaginary offers an innovative space for the female protagonists to articulate the psychosocial trauma embedded in and perpetuated by their neopatriarchal Symbolic orders, it fails to offer material solutions – as evidenced by the bleak endings of both narratives. Rima's oscillation between "writing" and illustrating her story, as well as her obsession with circles and the affective power of the senses, traps her in a circular logic where, as she states, "these things between writing and drawing and truth... they confuse me, they make me afraid."[72] In attempting to convey this fear to the reader, she says, "It builds traps for you in your body [...] and it is the shape of a circle, with no beginning and no end."[73] As previously stated, there is a circularity to storytelling, which troubles her. Midway through the narrative, she says, "I have to arrange the story for you [...] supposedly a story has a beginning and an end [...] so let's go back to the beginning."[74] She repeatedly circles what is for her the moments of greatest trauma, such as the death of her mother and her brother and Hassan's "disappearance." Furthermore, she is aware of these repetitions, telling the reader, "I told you these details a little earlier, you will feel I am repeating myself, but you are starting to know my theory now, about circular stories with intersecting centers which are only completed by retellings and new details."[75] Her anxiety peaks in the final pages, when she remains trapped in a basement, dying of starvation and the lingering effects of the chemical attack: "My stories aren't finished. [...] The story of my mother who disappeared. [...] The story of my brother who disappeared. [...] The story of Hassan, who disappeared. [...] I am a story, I, too, will disappear."[76] And with her final breath, she returns to the checkpoint scene at the start where her mother is killed: "We went out on a small bus. It was just a short journey, like ones we had made dozens of times before."[77]

Consequently, Rima's immersion in the Imaginary has not produced a resolution, as the narrative ends with her death while the war continues unabated. Paul Verhaeghe argues that while a subject may appeal "to the Imaginary in order to

---

characterized by neurotic obsessive compulsiveness. For more see Freud, Sigmund. *Moses and Monotheism* (Hogarth, 1932).
[72] Yazbek, 218.
[73] Ibid., 80.
[74] Ibid., 145.
[75] Ibid., 300.
[76] Ibid., 312-313.
[77] Ibid., 314.

deal with the Real," such attempts are "doomed to failure."[78] He illustrates how Lacan's register of orders is interrelated and deterministic, whereby it is expressed thusly: S > I > R. This configuration shows that the Symbolic order dominates the Imaginary and the Real. Consequently, given that the Imaginary is determined by the Symbolic, it will never produce a satisfactory resolution to the lack of the Symbolic.

Samman's protagonist appears to grasp this by the end of the narrative. As a writer who spent a decade calling for the revolution, which has now violently erupted, her central anxiety through the narrative concerns her culpability in the resulting carnage and whether the time has come for her to put down the pen and join the fight. Following several failed evacuation attempts, she is finally rescued from her flat and joins other survivors escaping the city. However, she leaves the relative safety of the convoy and walks to the beach. Here, she removes a gun from her satchel along with the pages of the manuscript she has been writing (which we have been reading). Looking at the gun, she admits, "There's no escaping the bullet when they leave you no other choice."[79] She then tucks the gun in between the pages of the manuscript, "like a child nestled in a womb," and lies down to contemplate her next steps.[80] The irresolution of the ending points to a recognition that there is no true refuge in the Imaginary. Metaphors and fables – such as those of the boy's birthday gifts – are insufficient. Convictions must be put into action, as when she suspects earlier in the narrative that "if I don't reconcile myself to death, to weapons, violence, and blood, I'll have no peace."[81] Furthermore, her acceptance of the gun, acceding to masculinist war logic, indicates a belief that violence is necessary to reconstitute, or "birth," a more just Symbolic order.

Conclusion

This chapter has argued that the protagonists of *Kawābīs Beirut* and *Planet of Clay* react to the utter breakdown of their social realities, or Symbolic orders, by seeking refuge in the fantasy-laden, visual field of the Imaginary. Both Rima and Samman's unnamed protagonist write their stories while witnessing the horrifying violence that surrounds them. Moreover, they are personally subjected to trauma such as chemical attacks, shootings, starvation, and witnessing the death of loved ones. Consequently, they evince traumatic responses such as compulsive repetitions and silence, which revert to Freudian understandings of trauma's effect on the psyche.

---

[78] Paul Verhaeghe, *Does the Woman Exist? From Freud's hysteric to Lacan's Feminine*, trans. Marc du Ry (Rebus Press, 1997), 41-42.
[79] Samman, 334.
[80] Ibid., 334.
[81] Ibid., 157.

However, by drawing on Lacan's register of orders, we can fruitfully engage with the protagonists' responses to the wider psychosocial implications of the respective wars that form the backdrops of these narratives. The civil wars have ruptured the Symbolic and revealed the traumatic Real, which I argue manifests as neopatriarchal hegemonic structures that continually generate war paradigms. As the Symbolic is a language-mediated order of signifiers, the protagonists display fundamental anxieties regarding the referential capacity of language in conveying traumatic experiences. Consequently, both protagonists retreat into the Imaginary. For Rima, this is reflected in her reliance on senses, colors, and shapes to narrate her story. Yazbek notes that in writing *Planet of Clay*, she had chosen "to remain in the realm of wonder to outstrip the violence of the story."[82] For Samman's protagonist, hallucinations, nightmares, and surreal encounters are the preferred modes for documenting her experiences. In both narratives, a semiotic, pre-symbolic dimension allows the protagonists to articulate trauma in a manner that eschews the violent discourse of men.

However, given its determination by the Symbolic, appeals to the Imaginary are doomed to failure. Both texts end on a bleak, irresolute note: Rima perishes of starvation, alone and abandoned, while Samman's protagonist seems to surrender to the logic of war in the hopes that it will produce true and lasting change in the psychosocial structures governing their reality. From our position in the present, knowing the Lebanese war lasted fifteen years. This may appear naive in light of how scholars of Arab war literature have noted the cyclical nature of political conflicts where a "patriarchal tribal system creates war, war is used to destroy the authoritarian system, war begets more war and violence."[83] However, considering the context of production for *Kawābīs Beirut* (which Samman completed in February 1976 and which was serialized in a Lebanese magazine until August of that year), at the time, such a supposition may have appeared plausible and, in its way, hopeful.

Bibliography

Accad, Evelyne. "Sexuality, War, and Literature in Lebanon." *Feminist Issues* 11, no. 2 (1991): 27-42.

Al-Samman, Hanadi. *Anxiety of Erasure: Trauma, Authorship, and the Diaspora in Arab Women's Writings.* Syracuse University Press, 2015.

Ball, Anna & Karim Mattar. "Dialectics of Post/Colonial Modernity in the Middle East: A Critical, Theoretical and Disciplinary Overview." *The Edinburgh Companion to the Postcolonial Middle East,* edited by Anna Ball and Karim Mattar, Edinburgh University Press, 2019, pp. 3-22.

---

[82] Inner fly-leaf of the first edition.

[83] Evelyne Accad, "Sexuality, War, and Literature in Lebanon," *Feminist Issues* 11, no. 2 (1991): 32.

Bou Ali, Nadia. *Psychoanalysis and the Love of Arabic: Hall of Mirrors.* Edinburgh University Press, 2020.

Britton, Celia. "Structuralist and Poststructuralist Psychoanalytic and Marxist Theories." *The Cambridge History of Literary Criticism,* Cambridge University Press, 1995, pp. 197-252.

Caruth, Cathy, ed. *Trauma: Explorations in Memory.* Johns Hopkins University Press, 1995.

Freud, Sigmund. *Totem and taboo: Resemblances between the psychic lives of savages and neurotics.* Ktoczyta.pl, 2020.

Kristeva, Julia. *The Kristeva Reader,* edited by Toril Moi, Blackwell, 1986.

Lacan, Jacques. "The Mirror Stage." *Reading French Psychoanalysis,* edited by Dana Birksted- Breen, Sara Flanders, and Alain Gibeault, Routledge, 2010, pp. 97-104.

——. *The Four Fundamental Concepts of Psycho-Analysis,* translated by Alan Sheridan, Penguin, 1994.

LaCapra, Dominick. *History in Transit: Experience, Identity, Critical Theory.* Cornell University Press, 2004.

——. "Trauma, Absence, Loss." *Critical Inquiry,* 25, 4, 1999, 696-727.

Noorani, Yaseen. "Normative Notions of Public and Private in Early Islamic Culture." *Harem Histories: envisioning places and living spaces,* edited by Marilyn Booth, Duke University Press, 2010, pp. 49-68.

Samman, Ghada. *Kawābīs Beirut.* 11th ed., *Manshurat Ghada al-Samman,* 2020.

Sharabi, Hisham. *Neopatriarchy: A Theory of Distorted Change in Arab Society.* Oxford University Press, 1992.

Verhaeghe, Paul. *Does the Woman Exist? From Freud's hysteric to Lacan's Feminine.* Translated by Marc du Ry, Rebus Press, 1997.

Yazbek, Samar. *Planet of Clay.* translated by Leri Price, World Editions, 2021.

Further Reading

Accad, Evelyne. Sexuality and War: Literary Masks of the Middle East. New York University Press, 1990.

Balaev, Michelle, ed. Contemporary Approaches in Literary Trauma Theory. Palgrave Macmillan, 2014.

Cooke, Miriam. War's Other Voices: Women Writers on the Lebanese Civil War. Cambridge University Press, 1987.

Craps, Stef. "Beyond Eurocentrism: Trauma Theory in the Global Age."The Future of Trauma Theory: Contemporary Literary and Cultural Criticism, edited by Gert Buelens, Sam Durrant, and Robert Eaglestone, Routledge, 2014, pp. 45-61.

——. Postcolonial Witnessing: Trauma out of Bounds. Palgrave Macmillan, 2013.

Craps, Stef, and Gert Buelens. "Introduction: Postcolonial Trauma Novels." Studies in the Novel, 40, 2008, 1–12.

Dalley, Hamish. "The Question of 'Solidarity' in Postcolonial Trauma Fiction: Beyond the Recognition Principle." Humanities, 4, 3, 2015, 369-392.

Durrant, Sam. Postcolonial Narrative and the Work of Mourning: J. M. Coetzee, Wilson Harris, and Toni Morrison. State University of New York Press, 2004.

Eng, David L. & David Kazanjian, eds. Loss: The Politics of Mourning. University of California Press, 2002.

Freud, Sigmund and Joseph Breuer. The standard edition of the complete psychological works of Sigmund Freud. Vol. 2 (1893-1895): Studies on Hysteria. The Hogarth Press & The Institute of Psychoanalysis, 1957.

Gilroy, Paul. Postcolonial Melancholia. Columbia University Press, 2004.

Hassan, Waïl S. "Postcolonialism and Modern Arabic Literature: Twenty-first-century Horizons." The Edinburgh Companion to the Postcolonial Middle East, edited by Anna Ball and Karim Mattar, Edinburgh University Press, 2019, pp. 43-56.

Kahf, Mohja. "The Silence of Contemporary Syrian Literature." World Literature Today, 75, 2001, 224-236.

Khanna, Ranjana. Dark Continents: Psychoanalysis and Colonialism. Duke University Press, 2003.

Luckhurst, Roger. The Trauma Question. Routledge, 2008.

Moore, Lindsey. Narrating Postcolonial Arab Nations: Egypt, Algeria, Lebanon, Palestine. Routledge, 2017.

O'Ballance, Edgar. Civil War in Lebanon, 1975-1992. Palgrave Macmillan, 1998.

Stocks, Claire. "Trauma Theory and the Singular Self: Rethinking Extreme Experiences in the Light of Cross-Cultural Identity." Textual Practice, 21, 1, 2007, 71–92.

Valassopoulos, Anastasia. Contemporary Arab Women Writers: Cultural Expression in Context. Routledge, 2007.

Ward, Abigail, ed. Postcolonial Traumas: Memory, Narrative, Resistance. Palgrave Macmillan, 2015.

Chapter 4

Speaking Trauma from within Catastrophe: Re-scripting Psychoanalysis in *The Search for Walid Masoud*

Nora E. H. Parr

University of Birmingham

Abstract

In his instantly canonical *The Search for Walid Masoud*, Palestinian author Jabra Ibrahim Jabra grapples with a definition of trauma that could make sense of the experience of Palestinian displacement. In typical Jabra fashion, however, 'making sense' is precisely what is done away with. Indeed, it is the sense of certainty, of categorization, that is challenged. By integrating the character of the Psychologist, even as he is derided and demonstrated as corrupt, the work introduces terms of psychoanalysis, creates a critical distance from them, adapts, and then transforms the vocabulary of trauma to fashion a unique schema of meaning. The novel represents something of a run-in: it juggles the hot topics of his Arab intellectual circles and personal/communal experiences of trauma. While the novel produces no definitive definition of trauma or final resolution on just how the use of the term is or is not colonial, it does give a foothold into a question that has often vexed contemporary scholars: how colonial or decolonizable is trauma theory?

Keywords: Palestinian Literature, trauma, psychoanalysis, decolonization, postcolonial

* * *

> In a world of terror, murder, hunger, and hatred, how can you find your inner psychological balance – or whatever you want to call it.
>
> Walid Masoud[1]

---

[1] Jabra, Ibrahim Jabra. *al-Baḥth ʿan Walīd Misʿūd: riwāya*, Beirut: Dār al-Ādāb,1978; Trans. Roger Allen, Adnan Haydar, Syracuse, NY, Syracuse University Press, 2000: 3. All quotations and thus page references refer to the translation, unless specified otherwise.

Jabra Ibrahim Jabra's *The Search for Walid Masoud (al-Baḥth ʿan Walīd Misʿūd: riwāya, 1978; Trans. Roger Allen, Adnan Haydar, 2000)* has been called many things: a retelling of "modern Palestinian history,"[2] "a critique of the political and cultural conditions in the modern Arab world,"[3] and a groundbreaking work of Arabic fiction. Beyond, or perhaps even within, these debates about the nation and culture of the 1980s, the work has much to say to current debates around trauma discourse and its colonial legacies.[4] To a field that is today grappling with whether and how global south experiences of harm can (or cannot) be articulated through a Euro-American language of psychology or diagnosed through the DSM V, this Palestinian novel adds a careful and nuanced view. It shows at once how language and knowledge histories are complex and interwoven, how assumptions about the structure of the mind in society shift across contexts, how the imposition of ideas can occlude an understanding of trauma, and also how adapted concepts can very much aid in the expression and communication of the experience of harm in non-western contexts.

Written by a Palestinian refugee from Bethlehem displaced to Baghdad (b. 1919, d. 1994), *Walid Masoud* captures the end of an era when decolonization was a practice and not a buzzword, but as hope for revolution waned. The novel

---

[2] David Tresilian, *A Brief Introduction to Modern Arabic Literature* (United Kingdom, Saqi Books, 2012): 102.

[3] Peter Issa, "In Search of Walid Masoud" in *World Literature Today* 75, no. 2 (2001): 404.

[4] Scholars have noted Jabra's interest in psychoanalysis, and indeed other works by the author also mention the field explicitly. However, the work has not been read in either critical tradition for its critical position on the field. See, for example: Franjiya, Bassam Khalil. *Al-lghtirāb fi-l-riwāya al-filasṭīniya* (Beirut: Muʾassasat al-abāhth al-arabiya, 2008); Arav, Mostsfa Mahdavi and Zainab Esmaeili. "[Arabic] Psychological Analysis of the Novel "In Search for Walid Masoud" by Focusing on Jung's Archetypes" in *Lisān-i Mubīn* 11, no. 38 (2019): 102-85; Hassan, Abu Shawish "[Arabic] Alienation in the novel *Looking for Walid Masoud* by Jabra Ibrahim Jabra," in *Journal of the Islamic University for Humanities Research* 14, no. 2 (June 2006), 121-169. For more explicit reference by Jabra to the field of psychoanalysis see his short story "Arak" (1956) where an earnest and non-corrupt character carries books on psychology around with him and insists that his reading of them is not a futile endeavor. More recently, Arabic Literary scholar William Tamplin, in carrying out research on the life and works of Jabra Ibrahim Jabra, suggested that new readings might be done of the author's work in light of historical evidence that showed his arrival in Bethlehem was the result of the Sayfo genocide in modern day Turkey. Tamplin has suggested that Jabra had embedded this family experience into his writing (if not his psyche), and that this, combined with what would be a second displacement and exile (the first based on religion, the second based on national identity) at the hands of Zionist forces during the Nakba, invites "Comparisons…with narratives of second- and third-generation Holocaust survivors, who have been shown to evince both a reticence about their families' trauma and the actual symptoms of prior generations' traumas." See Tamplin, William. "The Other Wells." *Jerusalem Quarterly* 85, no. 31 (2021): 30-60.

takes a stark look at the "world of terror, murder, hunger, and hatred" that the author found himself living in. Part of the work of the novel was to find a language to articulate that ugly world and what it felt like to exist as a part of it – knowing that the ugliness was only going to continue. Within this larger effort, a thread of the novel looks at psychoanalysis and asks Freud and the discipline that he galvanized if its language is capable of articulating the human response to a horrible world. This analysis is of the novel's question to Freud. In asking if psychoanalysis and the field of knowledge it catalyzed can articulate the pain of being Palestinian, the answer that *Walid Masoud* provides is no…and yet.

The search for Walid Masoud is, in fact, a search for a language of life-amid-ongoing-catastrophe. Thirty years after Palestine's Nakba, when 800,000 (including Jabra) were driven from their homes and villages; eleven years after the Nakba, when Israel expanded its territorial claims and surety of the success of a united Arab response ended; five years after the peak of Palestine's transnational solidarity,[5] the novel manages this by making catastrophe a sort of subject of analysis through the device of a detective's mission. The book, as the title suggests, really is the search for Walid. The middle-aged protagonist is missing from the work's opening pages, and it is his friends who set out to find him. As they retrace his steps, his friends first want to understand if Walid left of his own accord, if he was taken, if he was killed, and by whom. A refugee, a victim of torture at the hands of both Israeli and Iraqi governments, a Palestinian fighter, political organizer, and lover of many a culturally off-limits or married woman, his friends have a hard time assessing what elements of Walid's life put him most at risk. In this quest to find Walid – dead or alive – the friends must find a language to speak about the man's life and analyze his experience. It is not a coincidence that one of the friends gathered to help find Walid is a psychologist,

---

[5] In 1947/8 Zionist militias organized to clear Palestinians from their homes in what Israeli New Historians later uncovered as 'Plan Dalet'. The state of Israel was later declared and recognized, and boarders established so that displaced Palestinians could not return home. For more, see Morris, Benny. *1948: a history of the first Arab-Israeli war.* Yale University Press, 2008, and Pappe, Ilan. *The ethnic cleansing of Palestine.* Simon and Schuster, 2007. In 1967, following a failed attempt by a united Arab force to regain Palestinian territories, the Israeli army occupied the West Bank (administered by Jordan from 1948), Gaza Strip (nominally under Egyptian authority since 1948) and the Egyptian Sinai (the territory was later returned). The defeat was a crushing blow to Arab unity which was a dominant political aim. The loss changed the landscape of Mideast politics, and left Palestinians largely to fight for themselves. For more on the cultural impact of the loss of 1967 see: Kassab, Elizabeth Suzanne. *Contemporary Arab thought: Cultural critique in comparative perspective.* Columbia University Press, 2010. On Palestinian resistance and the rise of transnational solidarity which followed, see: Mogannam, Jennifer Marie. *Revolution Until Victory? Decolonizing Land, Nation and the People through Palestinian-Lebanese Transnational Resistance Praxis.* University of California, San Diego, 2019.

and one of the languages deployed in the search for what is missing is that of psychoanalysis. It is the deployment and adaptation of this language that this essay focuses on.

For Jabra and his character Walid, life had become synonymous with loss. All there was to articulate this loss at the time, however, was empty political rhetoric about the surety of revolution that few actually believed.[6] There was, and to some extent remains, a search for a language to capture and make this loss tangible. The harms experienced over, during, and across time largely defy available categorizations that tend to understand harm as time-limited.[7] As Palestinian writer and historian Sherene Seikaly reflected on the 75th anniversary of the Nakba, for Palestinians (and indeed for many), "violence and dispossession are not interruptions. They are markers of the temporal and spatial suspension that make up the every day."[8] This state of loss is where the story of *Walid Masoud* begins. It is within this state of loss that Walid exists. In the political discourse of post-67 in the Arab world, there was not really a language to express this position. There was still a degree of shock over the failure of Arab Unity, a shift toward support for the Palestinian resistance and its' notion of 'revolution until victory,' and a slow shift toward normalization (Egypt would sign a peace treaty with Israel the year after the novel was published). No one wanted to talk about failure, loss, or the increasingly oppressive tactics being employed to keep the status quo for those in power. How, then, is Walid's disappearance traced, which was surely related to this context of loss and oppression?

It is within this context that Walid's friends – including the psychologist Dr Tariq Raouf – gather in a private Baghdad garden. Though many of the assembled were leftists in their youth, middle age had brought its attachments to the status quo until the loss of their friend, a loss that shook them all into a search for Walid, for a language of finding him. Beyond a vaguely Marxist background, most of this friend group has a British or American education: some are bankers, others government officials, and most of the women had at some point been Walid's lover. This motley crew of peers – a neat representation of the Baghdad elite – join to find out where Walid has gone. The options generated by the group included being killed by the Israeli government, by the Iraqi government, by a jealous friend (there were two candidates), by a jealous ex-lover (or their husband or brother), and by suicide. Or, in the case that he is missing, he is

---

[6] See for example Kassab, *Contemporary Arab Thought* for an overview of the rhetoric of the era. See also Nouri Gana's *Melancholy Acts: Defeat and Cultural Critique in the Arab World.* New York: Fordham University Press, 2023.

[7] See, for example, Craps, Steph. Xx.

[8] Sherene Seikaly. "Nakba in the age of Catastrophe," *Jadliyya*, Nakba 75, published online May 15, 2023. Last accessed at: https://www.jadaliyya.com/Details/45037/Nakba-in-the-Age-of-Catastrophe on May 17, 2023.

missing in action: on a mission with the Palestinian resistance, captured and imprisoned by Israel on his way to visit his wife in the British asylum, or captured by hostile militias on a visit his son with the Palestinian fighters outside of Beirut. To discover his whereabouts, his peers dig into Walid's comings and goings, his affairs, his history of personal losses, and how each of these successive losses might have made him feel. It is in answering these questions that the friends deploy the terminology introduced into the text by Dr. Raouf, wondering if he had this or that delusion, complex [*aqda*], hysteria [*al-histīrīa*], sickness [maradh], or might benefit from a given treatment [*alāj*]. The friends do not use the words blindly or parrot Dr. Raouf's ideas. As the sections below work through, the characters ridicule the doctor, examine the ideas he presents, break down some of his underlying assumptions, and use the words in their unique ways in order to create a language for Walid and also for themselves.

In using a particular vocabulary to define and articulate a unique vision of the self/world relationship, the characters of *Walid Masoud* forge a language, or indeed a schema for language, that acknowledges the loss at the core of Walid's life. While this is the language for articulating the relationship of one man to his world in the novel, as a novel, *Walid Masoud* is rather finding a language for the Palestinian loss, or as Seikaly puts it, the loss that makes up "the everyday." Tracing the hows and whys of this process of adoption/translation/adaptation gives us insight into the colonial realities and decolonial potentials of psychoanalysis. However, the 'results' of an analysis of *Walid Masoud* are not, for many reasons, a model for where and how psychoanalysis can be deployed in the global south. This is because of context. What works, why, and how, for Walid, is far more connected to the place and time that Jabra wrote the text than any universal maxim on the decolonial potential of psychoanalysis. In order to draw out any larger lessons, it must first be acknowledged that the novel's mobilization of Freud's science has more to do with Jabra's understanding of the field and how he wove it into his fiction in the 40s, 50s, 60s, and 70s as he reached his literary peak. So psychoanalysis, as it is represented in the text, is a reflection of Jabra's understanding of it, which, as we can trace, was not insignificant. As an elite university student (of literature), Jabra was, for long stretches, totally immersed in the literature and discourse that surrounded the field. Still, he was not a student of psychology. He did make regular, if infrequent, references to different psychoanalytic terms in his critical writings, but perhaps nowhere as intensely as in *Walid Masoud*. For broader context, we can turn to the work of Omnia El Shakry, whose *The Arabic Freud* demonstrated that psychoanalytic terms and indeed the field of psychology–its terms and its foundational relationships to the human, their mind, and cosmology – were never 'directly' translated into Arabic. Rather, as she writes in her introduction, they were a "Translating and blending [of] key concepts from psychoanalysis with classical Islamic concepts…to produce a theory of the self that was at once in concert with and heterogeneous to European analytic thought."[9] So, it is important to note that any lines or distinctions between a 'western' or Arab/ic knowledge system, ideas of the mind and the self, are neither totally separate nor universally shared. Both are unstable categories, and findings here represent their intersection or a map of their relationship at a specific moment, which is the result of particular pasts.

There is no single body of 'the science of the mind' across either Anglo-European or Arabic-Middle Eastern systems. Michael Dols, in his foundational work on the concept of madness in Medieval Islam, traced a knowledge transmission (and translation) of ideas of the mind in Arabic to Greek theories of the mind, which were then translated into Syriac and from there into Arabic. This transmission "of medical learning from Syriac into Arabic was wholesale," Dols writes.[10] European medical thinking and psychoanalysis also owe a large debt to Greek thought, some of which were engaged based on the Greek sciences preserved by Arab-world scholars during the medieval era.[11] The intersections between knowledge systems were further entangled during the nineteenth-century archaeological (and indeed colonial) bonanza, where Europe set out to imagine its past by harvesting the history (and the artifacts) of the Middle East.[12] The issue of what knowledge belongs to who, then, is far more complicated than much of postcolonial discourse makes room for; this is not a context of identifying who made what, who claims what, and what was imposed or adopted by whom. Where the postcolonial fails, decolonial language has a little more scope for complexity. Rather than a separation of colonial and "indigenous" knowledge systems, the language of decolonization emphasizes systems of knowledge.[13] Or, as Gurminder K. Bhambra puts it, decolonization

---

[9] Omnia S. El Shakry, *The Arabic Freud: Psychoanalysis and Islam in Modern Egypt* (Princeton: Princeton University Press, 2017), 2.

[10] Michael W. Dols and Diana E. Immisch. *Majnūn: The Madman in Medieval Islamic Society* (Clarendon Press: Oxford University Press, 1992), 38.

[11] See: Wisnovsky Robert et al. *Vehicles of Transmission Translation and Transformation in Medieval Textual Culture* (Brepols, 2011).

[12] Yannis Hamilakis. "Decolonizing Greek archaeology: indigenous archaeologies, modernist archaeology and the post-colonial critique" in *A Singular Antiquity: Archaeology and Hellenic Identity in Twentieth Century Greece*, ed. Dimitris Damaskos and Dimitris Plantzos (Athens: Benaki Museum, 2008): 273-284; Downing, Christine. "Sigmund Freud and the Greek mythological tradition." *Journal of the American academy of religion* 43.1 (1975): 3-14. Claiming (or at least capturing) the historical knowledge of the ancient world did not stop at Greek thought. See Elliot Colla on the shift from the Greek to Egyptian, *Conflicted Antiquities: Egyptology Egyptomania Egyptian Modernity*. Durham: Duke University Press, 2007.

[13] See Gurminder K. Bhambra, "Postcolonial and decolonial dialogues" in *Postcolonial Studies* 17, no. 2 (2014): 115-121.

shifts the frame from a beginning with the colonial 'encounter' to one that considers "the broader histories of colonialism, empire, and enslavement."[14] This is the ground on which an investigation of the usage and adaptation of psychoanalytic language in *Walid Masoud* must begin.

Faithful to the lessons of context, it is important to place the present reading and its intervention into contemporary debates on trauma within a wider pursuit of the idea by Palestinian researchers and mental health practitioners, as well as peers doing research from and with other "global south" communities. For decades, Palestinian scholars have shown how a PTSD-informed language of mental health is insufficient for capturing the types, kinds, and magnitudes of non-western (or non-normative) experiences of harm[15] and demonstrated that existing methods of description fail to adequately assess diverse mental health conditions,[16] and fail – at the level of discourse – to provide an adequate imaginative path toward for "recovery."[17] Of course, twenty-first-century mental health interventions are not the same as a Freudian language of psychoanalysis (though work has shown the direct evolution of one into the other).[18] In parallel and in conversation with this criticism of existing modes are initiatives that see what Laura and Stephen Sheehi call the liberatory potential of psychoanalysis in Palestine. For the Sheehis and the many Palestinian analysts and analysands that they spoke with, psychoanalysis proved a language that made it possible to articulate the relationship between the self and the structures of power that repress it.[19]

There is agreement, then, on the problematic imposition of Western paradigms. Still, there is also a ready deployment of some of the tools and even discursive relationships of Western psychoanalysis and the psy-sciences. At the same time, at least some of this work replaces what Meari calls a victimization and resilience paradigm that underlies so many Western-innovated approaches with an idea of

---

[14] Ibid., 115.

[15] See Hogan W. Hammoudeh and R. Giacaman, "Quality of life, human insecurity, and distress among Palestinians in the Gaza Strip before and after the Winter 2008–2009 Israeli war" in *Quality of Life Research* 22, no.9 (2013): 2371-2379.

[16] See R. Giacaman, Y. Rabaia, V. Nguyen-Gillham, R. Batniji, R.-L. Punamäki, & D. Summerfield, "Mental health, social distress and political oppression: The case of the occupied Palestinian territory" in *Global Public Health* 6, no. 5 (2011): 547–559; and Mustafa Qossoqsi. *Intergenerational Psychosocial Effects of Nakbah on Internally Displaced Palestinians in Israel: Narratives of trauma and resilience*. Diss. (University of Essex, 2017).

[17] See L. Meari, "Reconsidering Trauma: Towards A Palestinian Community Psychology" in *Journal of Community Psychology* 43, no. 1 (2014), 76–86.

[18] See Dider Fassin and Richard Rechtman, *The Empire of Trauma: An Inquiry into the Condition of Victimhood,* trans. R. Gomme, (Princeton NJ: Princeton University Press, 2009).

[19] Lara Sheehi and Stephen Sheehi, *Psychoanalysis under occupation: Practicing resistance in Palestine*. Routledge, 2021, 4-6.

resistance. A reading of *Walid Masoud* finds a very similar – and much earlier – logic in relationship to Western-model psychoanalysis. What this reading of the work offers and adds to the field is an understanding of the gap between colonial imposition and Palestinian adaptation. Through the character of Dr. Raouf and the language of the mind that he introduces into the world of *Walid Masoud*, we can trace – perhaps be asked to trace – the origins of the language and how it is taken on and taken up by other characters. While the language does not, ultimately, find Walid, it does find a way of addressing his loss for those who remain.

Walid Masoud offers for today's field the beginnings of a look into the simultaneous truths of trauma theory's oppression and occlusion of Palestinian traumas and its invaluable adaptation in the articulation of these same experiences. This offers a foothold into a set of questions marked as urgent for contemporary scholars. These begin with: How colonial or decolonize-able is trauma theory? Is its application of the language of trauma the imposition of a limiting set of principles that make certain experiences of egregious harm invisible? Is the mobilization of the field's concepts and vocabulary a way toward recognition of the "suffering of the other"? Is there a way that ideas of trauma can be liberated from their colonial frameworks and put to use in the project of liberation? The novel, in a way, answers yes to each of these and crucially demonstrates why.

Divided into five uneven parts, this reading of Jabra's *Walid Masoud* first briefly shows how the language of psychology is brought into the world of the novel – through the derided and yet included Dr. Tariq Raouf. This section looks at how the corrupt, arrogant, and misogynist psychologist acts as the problematic "delivery mechanism" for a language of the mind. Through the doctor, the science and its language become tainted as representations of colonial-style control. A second section shows the operation of this language as a binary system of fixed or broken – or, as Meari put it, victim or resilient. It demonstrates this binary through the example of Walid's wife, Rima, who is committed to a British-run asylum in Bethlehem at the suggestion of Dr. Raouf after what is called a "breakdown." Next, we see how the language of control that Dr. Raouf introduced to his friends is reproduced, first to parrot and try and gain the power of this language, but then ultimately to mobilize its possibilities. This and the final section of analysis turn to Walid and his lovers, who take on elements of this science of the mind to re-craft tools that help them describe a broken world and a system of thought that makes it possible to live within it.

The "psychological balance" that Walid lamented in the quote that opens this paper is achieved precariously, and only once is the victim/resilience paradigm recognized as problematic and collapsed. In what seems an easy precursor to the developed modes of resistance through psychoanalysis, Walid crafts – and his lovers articulate – a language of the mind that must first enter an abyss. Rather than an idea of the victim, this language begins with the world that created victims, that world of "terror, murder, hunger, and hatred," and finds a way to resist being crushed by its reality.

A Controlling Science

Tariq al-Raouf obnoxiously throws out psychobabble, much of which his circle of elite and mostly Anglo-European-educated friends do not understand. When the group gathers, hot on the disappearance of Walid, to listen to his last words and try to collectively understand what might have happened, the best he can offer is that: "Walid, as Freud says, suffered from an Oedipal complex."[20] The comment stops what had been a relatively lively conversation in its tracks. Guests exchange miffed glances awkwardly until someone suggests they disperse for refreshments. When the evening ends, two of Walid's closest friends comment in frustration:

> I can't understand a thing. When everyone leaves, I'm going to look at a few books by Freud,
>
> To find out what the Oedipal complex is?
>
> Yes.[21]

These interjections are not infrequent. Tariq "diagnoses" Walid with any number of "complexes" ['aqdah/at] and his lovers with hysteria [al-histīrīa], sickness [maradh], treatment [alāj]. He has, for example, what Tariq describes as a "Don Juan complex," "a manifestation of a deep-rooted fear of losing his masculinity."[22] The doctor wields Jungian attachment theory, preferring it to Freud, who he also seems to use liberally, to try and get to the bottom of Walid, or more precisely, trying to decode and know Walid so he can become him. This is not professional curiosity.

In a direct reflection on the colonial origins of psychoanalytic frameworks,[23] Dr. Raouf wants to possess Walid. "I had to turn and turn around him in order to know

---

[20] Jabrā, Jabrā Ibrāhīm, *The Search for Walid Masoud: A Novel*, trans. Roger Allen and Adnan Haydar (Syracuse, NY: Syracuse University Press, 2000), 22. All quotes used in this chapter and page numbers refer to Allen and Haydar's translation, unless otherwise stated. When Arabic terms are included, they have been adapted from the first edition of Jabrā's *al-Baḥth ʿan Walīd Masʿūd: Riwāyah* (Beirut: Manshūrāt Dār al-Ādāb, 1978).

[21] Ibid., 24.

[22] Ibid., 129.

[23] See Ranjana Khanna, *Dark continents: Psychoanalysis and Colonialism* (Duke University Press, 2003).

a precious scrap of his reality,"[24] he reflects, believing somehow that to know Walid was to know "the mysterious forces that control man."[25] More accurately, however, Dr. Raouf is using the science of the mind because he wants to get what Walid has. Walid is a prolific lover, has slept with most of the wives or sisters of his friend group, and inspires a loyalty of affection that Tariq dreams of. His most direct access to Walid is through his wife, Rima, whom he treats as a psychologist, declares mad, and suggests institutionalization (a process the next section examines more closely). Walid is closely involved in the process. Tariq pursues everything else about Walid on his own, almost pathologically. He jumps at the chance to treat Walid's former lovers and spends a great deal of time trying to figure out who Walid has been involved with so he can pursue them as well. He does this first with Walid's published writing, trying to discern from it the secret of Walid's disposition. The near obsession leads Tariq's wife to quip: "Of course, I've read his book. But I didn't read it as if I were reading a coffee cup or telling fortunes the way you do."[26] He takes the same approach, however, with Walid's lovers.

Demonstrating the depths of Tariq's depravity – and the sheer gulf between the idea of psychological treatment and taking control of a person through manipulation of the promise of care – is his clinical abuse of Maryam al-Saffar. The abuse, Tariq recalls, "happened in the mid-sixties," when Maryam came seeking treatment for "insomnia and a headache that often lead to a kind of nausea."[27] The cause, he ascertained, was that the symptoms "sprang from her miserable relationship with her husband, together with what she called her 'attraction' to Walid."[28] Though he claims that he "never expected as I tried to minister to Maryam's sickness...that I'd find myself attracted to her," he mines their discussions, and later the journal that she shows him, for information on her relationship with Walid.[29] At one point, he had her journals copied without her permission so he could keep them in his files. As he later reflects more generally, his "long years of observation and listening to the confessions of patients...have led [him] to discover and learn a lot" about his patients, but particularly about Walid.[30]

Tariq's desire to possess goes beyond the intellectual. He shamelessly admits to himself that his relationship with her "is always mixed between obsession

[24] Jabrā, *The Search for Walid Masoud: A Novel,* 129.

[25] Ibid., 101.

[26] Ibid., 49. See also: Jabrā, *al-Baḥth 'an Walīd Mas'ūd: Riwāyah,* 68.

[27] Ibid., 108. See also: Jabrā, *al-Baḥth 'an Walīd Mas'ūd: Riwāyah,* 146.

[28] Ibid.

[29] Ibid., 111. See also: Jabrā, *al-Baḥth 'an Walīd Mas'ūd: Riwāyah,* 146.

[30] Ibid., 111.

and reality."[31] When he has the opportunity, the doctor does not hesitate to possess Maryam sexually. Spotting a window of opportunity, he recounts, he "led her into the examination room, where I made sure to close the door firmly," and has intercourse while she "kept saying 'no, yes, no.'"[32] He tries to maneuver the assault into an affair. Battling both anxiety and insomnia, Maryam calls Tariq late in the evening, and he advises her to take two sleeping pills, then invites himself over. When he arrives, she reluctantly opens the door, but the doctor thinks he hears Walid's voice in the background. Walid haunts Dr. Raouf; the more he studies him, the more Walid or the type of love he shares with the women in his life are elusive. It is, in fact, his obsession with possession that turns the man into the specter. Tariq's science – meant to know, order, and possess, only puts him farther from his goal. And while Walid largely rejects Tariq's imposition (when asked to confirm something for a diagnosis of Maryam, Walid categorically refuses, telling Dr. Raouf to base his assessment on his patient alone), he is forced to accept Tariq's vision of the world when it comes to Walid's wife, Rima.

A Binary System

Dr. Raouf serves as more than a vehicle for introducing a problematic epistemology of the mind. While he acts inappropriately with Maryam (and who knows how many other patients), his work with Walid's wife, Rima, is taken very seriously by everyone in the world of the novel. Dr. Raouf diagnoses Walid's wife – known both as Rima and Umm Marwan (mother of Marwan, their son) as having had a "nervous breakdown" (*inhiārrhā al-'aṣaby*: lit nervous system collapse) and encourages Walid's decision to take her to her family in Bethlehem or the British-run asylum there. While Dr. Raouf and his close friend (also largely discredited in the novel) Kazim are the only characters to call her "mad" (*majnūn*), there is a consensus among the characters that something has happened to Rima so that she is "gone... Gone."[33] In a novel that plays so openly with psychology and the mind, Rima acts as a fixed (yet unfixed) reference point. She represents at once the perception of a rigid and unhelpful system – the asylum where she ends up – and the inability of the knowledge of Dr. Raouf to even think about "treating" Palestinian trauma. In this system, an individual can either be "treated" or not. Rima cannot, and so in the system represented by Dr. Raouf, she is cast aside. In the world of Walid, as we shall later see, Rima represents a different sort of point of reference. For both systems, Rima has "collapsed," but what this means and how it fits into a larger schema of thought differs wildly. Before investigating what she represents, we first trace who she

[31] Ibid., 110.
[32] Ibid., 111.
[33] Ibid., 56.

is, what "happened," her position in the novel, and the language characters use to talk about her and her.

Rima's once-radiant-now-wan figure haunts both Walid and the novel. The two had married on one of Walid's visits to his family in Bethlehem and then departed for Baghdad. All had begun well enough. The two settled into life in Iraq and became even more integrated into the arts scene there. Rima had given birth to Marwan, their son. It was when Walid resumed his activities with the Palestinian resistance that Rima's "condition" emerged. As one character notes, Walid's frequent absences from Baghdad, as well as his detention by Iraqi authorities, "shook her with a deep shake [*hazat-ha hazan 'anīqan*] and disturbed her mind."[34] Everyone seems to agree that hers is a tragic but reasonable response to the realities of Palestinian life. She has lived through the Nakba, left her homeland for a life of exile, and her husband is constantly hunted by the authorities in both Iraq and occupied Palestine for his role as a resistance fighter/political organizer. The only words she utters on the subject of her mental state are to one of Walid's visiting friends. She tells him, wanly, that she is "tired, so very tired."[35] Dr. Raouf makes undescribed attempts to aid her and eventually recommends that she be sent to Bethlehem to either the asylum there or to her family. Both are, in essence, a form of palliative care.

The other characters in the novel similarly describe Rima as a sort of lost cause: "She was there, yet she wasn't there, looking yet seeing and hearing nothing."[36] Another character described what has happened to her as the "fall of her mind: (*maṣqtras-ha*)." This fall resulted in a sort of disappearance (notable, since the entire work is spent trying to "find" Walid, but Rima's disappearance seems a *fait accompli*) as one character described, "she was not alive so as to bless us with her company, and she was not dead so we could not forget her."[37] The intimation here is that in being dead, she could be mourned and somehow recuperated into society. As is, she has just disappeared, but without even a mystery to hold onto. Tariq and the world fashioned around his language give up on Rima and erase her from being. In the broader practice of the doctor, she forms one end of a sort of binary: some can be treated, and those who are hopeless. Rima is the latter. In the language developed by Walid and his lovers, as we see in the final section, however, Rima forms a different sort of conceptual anchor. No longer one side of a binary, she is the abyss beyond, a warning to fight, to remain, and a call for creativity within a delicate balance of mental well-being in a catastrophic situation.

---

[34] Ibid., 315.
[35] Ibid., 55. See also: Jabrā, *al-Baḥth 'an Walīd Mas'ūd: Riwāyah*, 76.
[36] Ibid., 110.
[37] Ibid., 110.

Before moving on, it is crucial to note that in the world of the novel, Tariq, the knowledge he wields, the British-run asylum in Bethlehem; these systems are only useful in the event of total collapse. Rima's condition is the only time in the work that the doctor is taken seriously, the only time Walid accepts his knowledge as valid. Of far more importance in the generation of an alternative, of a life beyond or before collapse, are the echoes of Tariq's language. How other characters take up, wield, or re-appropriate the ideas of the Oedipus complex, visions of masculinity or emasculation, of the realization of the self or its decimation; this is where an alternative is created. Thus, Tariq Raouf introduces the language of psychology into the novel. Hence, both readers and characters take his "science" with more than a pinch of salt and as of very limited relevance.

A Language Adopted

Derision, we see, is linked to the illusion of control or "knowing-ness" that Dr. Raouf wants his profession to provide. While at first, Tariq's peers scoff at his jargon. It is not long before we find the same words being mobilized. At first, and certainly for the male characters in the work, this language is used to try to understand what has happened to Walid. This is only a hair away from Dr. Raouf's usage, but it is an important distinction. Where Dr. Raouf sought to control for domination, his peers tried to use the language as a tool to find Walid. Where Rima's "disappearance" was not investigated, Walid's is – there is a sense that in understanding his psychological state, his friends can determine if he has killed himself, if he has been kidnapped, or if he has left Iraq for good to fight in the Palestinian resistance. In presenting the case of the missing Walid to his friends, one character comments, "I was aware that Walid, for all his notable success in his brokerage business, was going through a severe psychological crisis at the time," as if he thought this knowledge would help the group understand where Walid might be.[38] So, while characters put very little stock in Dr. Raouf as a specialist or someone who can understand the depths of Walid to the point of replication (and possession), they do use his language to engage in the search for their friend.

In their deployment of Dr. Raouf's terminology, Walid's friends, at times, replicate the sense of scientific knowledge and control that made it so useless for the doctor. They also tend, perhaps because they are amateurs, after all, to use the ideas tentatively and let their own experiences temper the language. One friend, who had just listened to an audiotape that Walid recorded while driving away from Iraq and left in a car on the roadside (his last known whereabouts), said, "Walid was going crazy when he recorded it. I agree with Tariq Raouf on that point. I don't care if it's an Oedipus complex or, more

---

[38] Ibid., 29.

obviously, straightforward madness."[39] The tape is transcribed -- by one of Walid's friends and into the text of the novel – so that the reader has direct access to Walid's last sort of testament. Scholars have spent quite some ink analyzing the imagined tape – a stream-of-consciousness diatribe with no clear structure or punctuation. Emily Drumsta describes it as a piece of writing where "content and form press at the limits of the reader's understanding, and it thereby aims to limn the process of sense-making itself."[40] It is significant, then, that another character says that the tape – beyond diagnosing madness – is a reflection of "a basic disposition in his psyche."[41] It is a powerful insight indeed that Walid's psyche pushes at the limits of "sense-making." We return to this again in the final section.

At some point in the search, Walid's friends also use the language of Dr. Raouf to examine their feelings about Walid. As one prominent member of the group reflects about another, he had "found in Walid the person whom he really, unconsciously, wanted to be, and whether that's why he clung to him so tenaciously" (however, this friend had not tried to gain access to the inner workings of Walid through psychological analysis of him and his lovers).[42] For many, the link to Walid was some sort of admiration. For these men, Walid represented the best of something that they aspired – or once aspired to be. Walid was and remained politically committed, while others had followed the typical pattern of rebellion in their youth, then (for some) quite a literal cooptation into government roles or positions at the bank. Somehow, while Walid retained a position at the Arab Bank (and by all accounts did quite well for himself), he remained intensely critical of all systems of oppression and homogenization, be they Zionist, governmental, or capitalist. For different reasons, Walid's closest friends reflected they retained their deep friendship with him because he reflected something they wished they had back at them.

Not all of the psychobabble is used to find Walid or understand the relationship between the missing man and his peers, however. It is also used amongst the men in Walid's circle to compete, put each other down, and criticize how the men choose to live and behave. One character derides another, tossing off a critical review he wrote of Walid's book in the local paper as the result of "a persecution complex: that's what's bothering Kazim."[43] Once Dr. Raouf's language became familiar, his monologues about Walid and how he will "lose

---

[39] Ibid., 271.
[40] Emily Lucille Drumsta, *Chronicles of Disappearance: The Novel of Investigation in the Arab World, 1975-1985* (University of California, Berkeley, 2016): 41.
[41] Jabrā, *The Search for Walid Masoud: A Novel*, 26.
[42] Ibid., 58.
[43] Ibid., 51.

his masculinity [*yufaqad rujulatuhu*]"[44] if he continues pursuing women as he does, illicit eye rolls – not because his language is nonsense but because his friends now assume that the diagnosis is not of Walid but of Tariq himself. The language remains a tool for belittlement, for cutting others down through this pretense of power and superiority through diagnosis, despite being used for genuine analysis and reflection.

While it is at times used in the service of finding Walid or understanding the relationship between him and the friends who miss him most, the use of Dr. Raouf's clinical language tends toward a sense of competition and comparison, fault and defect. For while it produces some interesting introspection, the language as it is mobilized here produces no results: it neither finds Walid nor does it find what is lost in any of his friends. In the hands of Walid himself and the minds and mouths of his lovers, the language of the mind is used to articulate deep feelings of love and loss. This usage ultimately adapts the schema and system of knowledge that the language relates to and creates a new relationship between the self, its failings, and a failed world.

A Language Adapted

As the words and concepts bandied about by Dr. Raouf became the language of the friend group, the words and the links they conjured between mind, body, and society were mobilized by a different set of characters to access and tell a different sort of story. Rather than a language of control on the lips and in the minds of Walid and his lovers, the language of psychology articulates deep feelings of love, loss, and trauma. Rather than the brutal binary of broken and fixed, it is a language of coping – of resistance – or, as Meari called it, *sumud* (steadfastness).[45] The characters have learned that they exist, as Walid puts it in the quote that opened this chapter, "in a world of terror, murder, hunger, and hatred." The language of psychology is used not only to describe the state of being in an ongoing catastrophe but also to achieve "psychological balance."[46] The vocabulary of all this grappling is pulled from the jargon of Dr. Raouf; just what is being balanced, even what balance means, is developed by the characters in and for their context.

In the world of *Walid Masoud*, the idea of balance begins with its failure and the abyss that awaits the individual, unable to cope with the dark realities of the time. Prefiguring what contemporary mental health experts repeat about the situation in Palestine today, that it is the "situation that is sick" and not the individuals, the idea of collapse in this schema of psychological balance is

---

[44] Ibid., 174.
[45] Meari, 67.
[46] Jabrā, *The Search for Walid Masoud: A Novel*, 3.

established as Walid undergoes a second round of torture at the hands of the Israeli military. "The critical thing," Walid thought as he was beaten, burned, and starved, "is not to break down. It's enough that Rima's had a breakdown, that she's living the life of the dead in a clinic...I'm going to die, I told myself, but I must not break down."[47] Failure, again, is not death. It is breakdown. And not just in the context of horrific physical torture but the insecurity and uncertainty that Rima lived with. This is, to be sure, describing the reality of Palestinian life, but it goes beyond.

The abyss, the "sick" situation, might afflict Palestine most obviously, but Walid observes it as an issue far beyond any single nation. As he reflects in the days after his torture:

> From the Arab Gulf to the Atlantic Ocean, I heard cries, I heard weeping, and the sound of sticks and plastic hoses. Capitals and Casbahs, the secret police were everywhere, and on mountain peaks and in the valleys below. Men in neat civilian suits walking to and fro like a thousand shuttles in a thousand looms, taking away to the centers of darkness people by the tens and hundreds, losing them in labyrinths of cellars and dungeons, and night and day the sound of questions, denial, and confession could be heard, the noise of rubber coming down on naked flesh; accusations and calumnies pile up in dossiers, and people's mouths fill with blood. How can I ever learn all that and come to accept it as a part of life?[48]

Having been imprisoned by Israeli forces and in his new home, Iraq, having mobilized for resistance across Europe and perhaps further afield, Walid becomes aware of the gruesome realities of his present. Every capital, every casbah, as he puts it, operates in the same way against those who would resist them. It is a reality from which there is no escape, only collapse. Here, the idea of collapse conjured by Rima is fleshed out. Her collapse is almost logical, given the enormity of the forces pressing down. But for Walid, who has seen the collapse and what the world of collapse looks like, he can only repeat, "the important thing is not to break down. People break down; I'm not made of steel, but I won't break down."[49]

The idea of breakdown is not, then, what Dr. Raouf and his system of diagnosis had meant. For him, Rima was untreatable, would not respond to his ministrations, and so should be sent for a sort of palliative care in an asylum. For Tariq, some people will respond to treatment, and those who will not, people whose minds can be "known" and organized, and those whose cannot. In *Walid*

---

[47] Ibid., 184.
[48] Ibid., 188.
[49] Ibid., 185.

Masoud, some people cannot bear the weight of the world, those who do not see the world as it is, and those who fight for the "psychological balance" to withstand it. The idea of breakdown is adapted to a new context. The rest of Dr. Raouf's language of the mind is used to create strategies to find and maintain a precarious balance within the abyss, a balance that sees the world as what it is and finds a way to avoid being crushed.

Living in the Abyss

Through Rima and his experiences of displacement and torture, Walid forges an architecture of "psychological balance" that requires first recognizing and positioning work within the existence of the abyss. Walid himself may have had a language for this, but this is not fleshed out as a process within the novel. What the work does represent is the repeated grapplings of his lovers, who encounter this psychic position. They do not leave Walid without seeing, in a sense, the abyss he lived within and having seen it. They must use what they learned of life with him to find their balance. In articulating it, they use the words of Dr. Raouf but for a purpose that seems well beyond the doctor's imaginative capacity. In the language of the novel, the difference in approach is articulated as one of control versus love. When Dr. Raouf tried to use his tools to dissect, diagnose, and control, Walid's lovers, as Wisal describes it, "got to know Walid from the inside" and came to an understanding through connection and desire.[50]

In their desire for Walid, his lovers became what Sheehi and Sheehi called "desiring subjects, even under the most suffocating violence."[51] Rather than subjects of analysis, the relationship with Walid opens up what the Palestinian clinicians that Sheehi and Sheehi interviewed called a "space" of unity and "consensual and negotiated relationships" that can "amplify the relationship between the psychic, the social, and the political."[52] Or, as Wisal puts it:

> I traveled along his mental orbits and his psychological and emotional ones as well. I started to know and to love him; I began to feel jealous. Time and again, the illusion came to me that Walid was actually me. I began knowing and loving him as I did my own self.[53]

In drawing out the difference between Tariq's clinical and abusive relationship with Maryam and Walid's relationship with his successive lovers, a difference is made clear between Tariq's search for control and Wisal's draw toward a space

---

[50] Ibid., 199.
[51] Sheehi and Sheehi, 5.
[52] Ibid.
[53] Jabrā, The Search for Walid Masoud: A Novel, 199.

of personal evaluation. While Wisal admits feeling jealousy when she is not with her lover, she eventually takes everything she has learned from Walid and uses it for her own benefit. After Walid (as Tariq angrily observes), his lovers move differently, more confidently – and more independently – within their world.

Just how this transformation happens is elaborated on by another lover, Maryam, who similarly describes the experience of loving Walid. It is a collapse, but not into the abyss. It is a breakthrough into the world where the abyss is recognized and where everything is done on its precipice. As Maryam recalls:

Walid, you are terrible! You are a curse! Curse! You shattered me! Pulverized me! I want you, I desire you, I'll kill you, I will take from you a small bit and I will eat each bit of you... [and I fell into his arms]...and I burst with tears and screams that I had not cried the like of in my life and my body rose up with a sacrificial convulsion and he held me with strength between his arms, and I shook and moaned in a terrifying euphoria [*nashwa ra'ba*].[54]

Here, there is that same idea of an end, "You shattered me! Pulverized me!" Maryam convulses out of whatever world she inhabits and into the world of Walid, which she enters with a "terrifying euphoria." One has to arrive at collapse, at destruction, and then see the world. The world that Maryam puts together links several key ideas. These are collected around the symbol of a rock. It is this creation of finding words and images that help her to make sense of a newly discovered psychology. Crucially, Walid takes Maryam to Palestine – and this is perhaps why Maryam gets further in her articulations than any of his other lovers.

She goes and wanders to the churches on the old streets and sees the refugee camps. It is her use of the language of Dr. Raouf here that clues a reader into the fact that she is building an idea of the mind with what she observes. Of the camp, she says: "For all its repressed nervousness, it had a semblance of organization, a strange organization, with children roaming everywhere."[55] The camp and its psychic energy hold meaning, which she talks about with Walid. He tells her that the stone houses in the camp, the stones of the old city, are where the revolution is happening: "Revolutionary cells are bouncing in every alley of this stone (*ṣakhūr*)."[56] The rock here is invested with important meaning. On a later triste to the mountains outside of Beirut, Maryam runs out of the villa into the garden naked, scratched by plants and bushes, "him

---

[54] Ibid., 226.

[55] Ibid, 233.

[56] Ibid., 233. Most of the camp homes by the 1970s were made at best of cinder block with asbestos or tin roofs, with construction already having begun to turn areas from these semi-permanent buildings to the more permanent cement homes that exist today. The novel nonetheless uses the work ṣakhr.

watching my madness laughing" and brings back a rock (*al-ṣahkra*).[57] As Drumstra has observed, "Maryam connects with the primal element of stone and experiences a loss of the self in nature," even more than this she enters "The world of mystical experience, where what is sensed overwhelms and defies rational judgment and categorization, and where the power relations between sensing subject and sensed object are destabilized."[58] In fact, in this destabilization she allows herself to be "pulverized" and to see the abyss that Walid has seen. In desiring him, she desires to be a (desiring) self within their dyad.

Maryam devotes the rest of her life (so far as we know it) to thinking through what the rock – which Walid so invested with revolutionary potential – means. The rock, that weight she picks up in the mountain garden, is the abyss. It is what the homes and camps of Bethlehem are made out of, the reality of Palestine and Palestinians.[59] This is dwelling literally within the abyss, within the breakdown. At some point, after the end of her marriage, after she has stopped seeing Walid and has gone on to study history and write a monograph – but before writing her own works of fiction – she goes to Dr. Raouf. She continues to try and find language to describe and explain herself and the world as she sees it. She presents Tariq with a series of notebooks wherein she has written down her attempts to understand the rock. She nearly literally hands Tariq the abyss for assessment. He is useless. We saw earlier his perspective. He had his secretary copy her notebooks so he could mine them for the secrets of Walid, and then he sexually assaulted Maryam. As she narrates the experience:

> When I put it [the rock] between the hands of the psychiatrist Dr. Tariq Raouf, it didn't lighten and it didn't budge, rather it transformed into many rocks, like a dragon whose head you cut off only to grow back two heads and then turn into two dragons, continuing every time you cut off one of its heads, it grows two more.[60]

The rock and the system of Dr. Raouf are not compatible – they are maybe even antagonistic. With the secrets to Walid in his hands, all he can see is the potential for knowledge as control. He makes a victim out of Maryam, who leaves the encounter feeling only pity for Tariq's wife.

---

[57] Ibid., 228.

[58] Drumsta, 37-38.

[59] It seems useful and important to also note that Jabra has chosen ṣakhr, not ḥajr as in "atfal al-hijara" or children of the stones as they came to be known during the first intifada ten years after the novel was published. The Arabic entomology connects ṣakhr with earth and a material of the earth, whereas ḥajr carries the meaning of blockage, limitation. See Hans Wehr, *A Dictionary of Modern Written Arabic* (Wiesbaden, Germany: Otto Harrassowitz Verlag, 1979): 185, 590.

[60] Jabrā, *The Search for Walid Masoud: A Novel*, 237.

The assumptions buried in Tariq Raouf's language are unequivocally disqualified from utility: utility in finding Walid, in gaining control over his life or memory, in providing the world of *Walid Masoud* with a method of understanding themselves and their world. However, adapted within the context and fashioned within the abyss, this becomes a useful language for the desiring self. It is a language and a schema of thought that Walid's lovers take on into successful and meaningful lives. Where most of the men in the novel remain jealous – lost in systems they don't believe in, or searching for meaning up unclear pathways – Maryam, Wisal, Jinan, and others use their new language of desire-in-catastrophe to find meaning. Whereas before, many of his lovers were in abusive or dead marriages or had no vocation or purpose, by the close of the novel, we understand them to be the hope that is holding the friend group together. Maryam, for her part, leaves her husband and finds love "like a 'collapsing damn' (*inhar al-sad*)," intimating the same dyadic relationship of space for love-in-catastrophe as she had with Walid.[61]

The relative "psychological balance" that his lovers find, however, *is* relative. At the close of the novel, Maryam asks herself about the rock/abyss:

> Why does it stay always a symbol in front of me, a beautiful tempting mystery, a fraught symbol in all that is not possible to put into all of the important/significant words, trying year after year? I saw it grow and grow and become a mountain, and I'm at its summit, hanging onto it, with whirlwinds of desire grabbing at me. And I've seen it get smaller and smaller, subsiding onto the bed, and shrinking further so I look for it, I want to take hold of it, and it slips away between my fingers.[62]

The rock is not something that goes away, not something that is balanced. The rock is the constant, the thing that creates the gravity, the laws of physics within which balance – or perhaps better, being – might be achieved.

Bibliography

Bhambra, Gurminder K. "Postcolonial and Decolonial Dialogues." *Postcolonial studies* 17, no. 2 (2014): 115-121.

Dols, Michael W and Diana E Immisch. *Majnūn: The Madman in Medieval Islamic Society.* Oxford: Oxford University Press, 1992.

Drumsta, Emily Lucille. *Chronicles of Disappearance: The Novel of Investigation in the Arab World, 1975-1985.* Berkeley, CA: University of California Press, 2016.

El Shakry, Omnia S. *The Arabic Freud: Psychoanalysis and Islam in Modern Egypt.* Princeton, NJ: Princeton University Press, 2017.

---

[61] Ibid., 215.
[62] Ibid., 228.

Issa, Peter. "In Search of Walid Masoud." *World Literature Today* 75, no. 2 (2001): 404.

Jabrā, Jabrā Ibrāhīm. *al-Baḥth ʿan Walīd Masʿūd: riwāyah.* Beirut: Manshūrāt Dār al-Ādāb, 1978.

—. *In Search of Walid Masoud: A Novel.* Translated by Roger Allen and Adnan Haydar. Syracuse, NY: Syracuse University Press, 2000.

Meari, L. "Reconsidering Trauma: Towards A Palestinian Community Psychology." *Journal of Community Psychology* 43, no. 1 (2014), 76–86. https ://doi.org/10.1002/jcop.21712.

Seikaly, Sherene. "Nakba in the age of Catastrophe," *Jadliyya*, Nakba 75, published online May 15, 2023. Last accessed at: https://www.jadaliyya.com /Details/45037/Nakba-in-the-Age-of-Catastrophe on May 17, 2023.

Sheehi, Lara, and Stephen Sheehi. *Psychoanalysis under occupation: Practicing resistance in Palestine.* New York: Routledge, 2021.

Tresilian, David, *A Brief Introduction to Modern Arabic Literature.* London: Saqi Books, 2012.

Wehr, Hans. *A Dictionary of Modern Written Arabic.* Wiesbaden, Germany: Otto Harrassowitz Verlag, 1979.

Further Reading

Arav, Mostsfa Mahdavi and Zainab Esmaeili. "[Arabic] Psychological Analysis of the Novel 'In Search for Walid Masoud' by Focusing on Jung's Archetypes." *Lisān-i Mubīn* 11, no. 38 (2019): 102-85.

Colla, Elliot. *Conflicted Antiquities: Egyptology, Egyptomania, Egyptian Modernity.* Durham: Duke University Press, 2007.

Downing, Christine. "Sigmund Freud and the Greek Mythological Tradition." *Journal of the American Academy of Religion* 43, no. 1 (1975): 3-14.

Fassin, Dider, and Richard Rechtman. *The Empire of Trauma: An Inquiry into the Condition of Victimhood* (R. Gomme, Trans.). Princeton, NJ: Princeton University Press, 2009.

Franjiya, Bassam Khalil. *Al-lghtirāb fi-l-riwāya al-filasṭīniya.* Beirut: Muʾassasat al-abāhth al-arabiya, 2008.

Giacaman, R., Rabaia, Y., Nguyen-Gillham, V., Batniji, R., Punamäki, R.-L., & Summerfield, D. Mental health, social distress and political oppression: The case of the occupied Palestinian territory. *Global Public Health* 6, no. 5 (2011): 547–559. https://doi.org/10.1080/17441692.2010.528443.

Hamilakis, Yannis. "Decolonizing Greek Archaeology: Indigenous Archaeologies, Modernist Archaeology and the Post-colonial Critique." *A Singular Antiquity: Archaeology and Hellenic Identity in Twentieth Century Greece.* Edited by Dimitris Damaskos and Dimitris Plantzos, 273-284. Athens: Benaki Museum, 2008.

Hammoudeh, W., Hogan, D., & Giacaman, R. "Quality of Life, Human Insecurity, and Distress Among Palestinians in the Gaza Strip Before and After the Winter 2008–2009 Israeli War." *Quality of Life Research 22,* no. 9 (2013): 2371–2379. https://doi.org/10.1007/s11136-013-0386-9.

Hassan, Abu Shawish "[Arabic] Alienation in the novel *Looking for Walid Masoud* by Jabra Ibrahim Jabra." *Journal of the Islamic University for Humanities Research* 14, no. 2 (2006): 121-169.

Khanna, Ranjana. *Dark Continents: Psychoanalysis and Colonialism.* Durham, NC: Duke University Press, 2003.

Qossoqsi, Mustafa. *Intergenerational Psychosocial Effects of Nakbah on Internally Displaced Palestinians in Israel: Narratives of trauma and resilience.* PhD diss. University of Essex, 2017.

Tamplin, William. "The Other Wells." *Jerusalem Quarterly* 85, no. 31 (2021): 30-60.

Wisnovsky, Robert et al. *Vehicles of Transmission Translation and Transformation in Medieval Textual Culture.* Turnhout, Belgium: Brepols, 2011.

Chapter 5

Messianic Remnants and Beasts of the Southern Wild

Concetta Principe

Trent University

Abstract

Giorgio Agamben argues that the exception of camp is the *Muselmann*; it exacts an ethical imperative for the survivor to bear witness. Agamben names the exchange between the Muselmann and the witness as the "messianic remnant." In Lacanian terms, Agamben's "messianic remnant" would be indicative of the messianic fantasy pointing to the "real" of the death camps, otherwise defined as the trauma of Auschwitz. What does this mean for Hushpuppy, the protagonist who promises to save her community from the global crisis in *Beasts of the Southern Wild*? Using Lacan and Agamben's insights, this chapter argues that what stands out about her messianic representation is that she is not only the exception but also the exception to the exception. She is a Black person in the bayou. More importantly, she is an exception to the messianic expectation of a grown man. If we, as audience members, are witnesses of Hushpuppy, the exception, then in whose interest is the messianic expectation in this film? That is, whose trauma is on display? In analyzing the film, I will show that the putative Black savior fantasy on screen is riddled with the white American trauma that sustains America's racist history in disturbing ways.

Keywords: Lacan, Agamben, the exception, trauma, messianic, *Beasts of the Southern Wild*, global warming, racism

* * *

Benh Zeitlin's *Beasts of the Southern Wild (2012)* seems to be a film about the trauma of the climate crisis, indicated by the story of a community in the "Baths" suffering extreme weather conditions. Yet if we consider the role of Hushpuppy, the protagonist, a young black girl living in the "Baths," we would suppose black racial trauma is driving the film. As a girl living in the Bayou, an encampment outside mainstream America, she brings to mind Giorgio Agamben's socio-political figure of the exception, the one who lives outside the city in the camps and can be killed with impunity. In *Remnants of Auschwitz*,

Agamben identifies the *Muselmann* as a double exception: not only does he exist outside the city in the death camp known as Auschwitz, but he also stands outside the social network of the camps as the most abject inmate, the one who was so diminished by hunger that he could barely walk, or talk, and whose death would go unnoticed. This extreme abjection is what survivor Primo Levi described as the horror of the figure: we do not want to look, but we must look. Levi's response inspires Agamben to theorize that the demand by the *Muselmann* for the survivor to bear witness is full of the potential of redemption, indicated in Agamben's naming that exchange as the "messianic remnant."[1] I have argued elsewhere that Agamben's theologico-political interest in the *Muselmänner* – his witnessing of the death camp inmate – points to what Lacan would define as the fantasy of trauma. In Agamben's case, the trauma is the psychic impact of the Nazi's systematic murder of millions of European Jews by those who survived.[2]

According to Lacan, trauma is the subject's "encounter" with the real, which generates the remainder known as the *objet a*, the bit of truth of the trauma. This truth is used to build the "fantasy," a narrative of sorts that is less about fictionalizing the trauma than it is about marking it so as to work through it.[3] In other words, Agamben's "messianic remnant" is the fantasy generated by the *objet a* of the real of the death camps, or the real "cut" that inspires naming the abject figure the *Muselmann*. In Zeitlin's film, Hushpuppy is similar to the *Muselmann* in

---

[1] Giorgio Agamben, *Remnants of Auschwitz: The Witness and the Archive*, trans. Daniel Heller-Roazen (New York: Zone Books, 2002), 159.

[2] See the chapter "The Messianic Exception" in my monograph *Secular Messiahs and the Return of Paul's Real: A Lacanian Approach* (169-182), for details of the role of the exception as the *objet a* of trauma, which Agamben uses to generate his idea of salvation as a bond between the exception and the survivor.

[3] Jacques Lacan adapted the principle of trauma from Freud's work in "Beyond the Pleasure Principle". In that essay, Freud uses various examples to show that the traumatic event is evident only in compulsive behavior, such as the child's *for-da* game which Freud understood as the child's way to organize the trauma of mother's departure. Lacan reconstitutes Freud's trauma with very particular terminology that relies on what he denotes are the three registers of psychic life: the imaginary, associated with the mirror stage; the symbolic, associated with language; the real, associated with the unknowable, radical and even transcendent element of life. Lacan redefines trauma as the subject's encounter with the 'real'. The impact of this encounter is the remainder, or the *objet a*. The subject's relationship to the *objet a* generates the 'fantasy,' a term that stands as the symbolic organization of the trauma, and indicates the unconscious compulsion of repetitive behavior such as the *for-da* game. Agamben's relationship to the *objet a* of the *Muselmann*, which is the remainder of the encounter with the 'real' of Nazi violence, manifests a 'fantasy' for redemption, or the 'messianic remnant'. Note that 'fantasy' is a symbolic organization of the trauma: it fails to be the trauma, or even tell us what the trauma was, in that it simply stands for that trauma. For more details on Lacan's treatment of the *objet a* and fantasy, see his *Seminar XI*.

that she is an exceptional exception. She lives in the "Baths," a community of social misfits that exists outside state jurisdiction; she is racially an exception to America's white hegemony, and considering her savior role in the film, her gender places her as the exception to the masculine salvation narratives. Suppose Hushpuppy can share so many predicates with the Muselmann. In that case, I suggest it is worth adapting Agamben's notion of the dynamic between the exception and the witness, or Hushpuppy and us – her audience – to explore the material of the "messianic remnant" operating in the film.

If we, as audience members, are witnesses of Hushpuppy, the exception, then in whose interest is the messianic expectation in this film? That is, whose trauma is on display? This is to say that, since the film is focused on a young Black girl fighting global warming, one would suppose that the film is in the interest of America's racial minority and or emblematic of a racial trauma from the perspective of American Black people. In analyzing the film in the pages ahead, I will show that the putative black savior fantasy on screen is riddled with the White American trauma that sustains America's racist history in disturbing ways.

The Remnant

In Lacan's terms, trauma is only evident in the symbolic organizing principle of the fantasy. The fantasy itself is always grown from, or built on, an element of the "encounter with the real" (the trauma) and has been defined as the "*objet a.*" The Holocaust is a recognizable trauma for Western citizens, and the effort to organize that trauma has been apparent in the simple function of sharing stories organized around recognizable figures that pointed to the real of the "*objet a.*" For example, Spiegelman's *Maus I* and *II* explores the art of survival in the camps in the benign image of a cat and mouse. Claude Lanzmann's epic documentary, *Shoa*, embodies the trauma of the camps through the geography, or literally the ground, of the death camps. In this company, Giorgio Agamben's *Muselmann* may be seen as the organizing fantasy of the "real" or "*objet a*" of Auschwitz that inspires his messianic fantasy, derived from Paul of Tarsus's revision of the Isaianic principle of the "remnant": "And Isaiah cries out concerning Israel, 'Though the number of the children of Israel were like the sand of the sea, only a remnant of them will be saved.'"[4] If, for Paul, the source of the remnant is this promise of Israel in the population of Jesus' followers, in Agamben's treatment of the fantasy, the messianic "remnant" spreads to include not people but anything that can be associated with "now" time: "in the time of now, there is a remnant according to the election of grace."[5] Whereas Paul's remnant represents both Jews and non-Jews as the followers of Jesus, Agamben's theologico-

---

[4] Rom. 9.27-29
[5] Agamben, 163.

messianic concept[6] expressed in "what remains between" the *Muselmann* and the survivor indicates a moment when the two are caught by each other.[7] This bond embodies the trauma we can read being worked through in Agamben's project.

Agamben's source for the *Muselmann* and the witness was drawn from the writing of Holocaust survivor Primo Levi. In his memoir, Levi reflects on his experience witnessing the most abject inmate of the camps: "Their life is short, but their number is endless; they, the *Muselmänner,* the drowned, form the backbone of the camp, an anonymous mass, continually renewed and always identical, of non-men who march and labor in silence, the divine spark dead within them."[8] If the *Muselmann* did not die from dysentery or starvation, he was destined to be chosen for the gas chambers. The fact this figure could not see his death coming, and so far, it was for Levi the most horrifying expression of death before death. This paradox, you might say, was the "real encounter" that inspired the naming of the abject inmate. In Agamben's treatment of the *Muselmann* figure, the horror is secondary to what Levi's experience attests to: the injunction to bear witness. Thus, Levi's fantasy becomes, for Agamben, the fantasy of the messianic remnant, each pointing to a different trauma.

Agamben formulates a messianic promise of the future by focusing on the ethical demand of witnessing. The promise centers on the connection between the inmate and the witness by associating Paul's "election of grace" with "the non-coincidence of the whole." By non-coincidence, we are to understand that the messianic quality of the remnant is meant to be a composite not of the Judeans or the Jesus followers but of Paul's notion of "now time." Agamben uses this principle of time as Walter Benjamin has defined it as neither in the historical temporal sense nor even in the divine eternal sense, but in the disjunction between these two times: that time which is of neither or against both. Agamben's disjunction of time means to include everything "outside time." Analogously, we can suppose that Agamben means that 'non-coincidence' references everything outside of coincidence. What is important about Agamben's nimble fusing of "disjunction of time" with "non-coincidence of the whole" – a kind of crossing that we find in the weaving of "fabric" – is that the messianic is human-made, not divinely sent, and is particular to the relationship between the witnesses (of the *Muselmann*) and the *Muselmann* (who cannot witness himself). Together, they "are neither the dead, nor the survivors, neither the drowned nor the saved. They are what remains between them," and in that sense, reference what is beyond these particulars as the "non-

---

6 Ibid., 162.

7 Ibid., 164.

8 Primo Levi, *Survival in Auschwitz: The Nazi Assault on Humanity*, trans. Stuart Woolf (New York: Simon and Schuster, 1996), 90.

coincidence of the whole."[9] This is to say that, in the act of witnessing what cannot witness for itself, the qualities of subjectivity (dead, survivor, drowned, saved) are sublimated in the dynamic of testimony: in returning speech to the speechless, testimony returns life to the dead, defying mortality's limit in temporal and eternal terms.[10]

In the relationship between the *Muselmann,* whose subjectivity has been reduced to a pure being, and the survivor, who has speech in the face of the impossibility of speech, Agamben's remnant can be seen as a conservative project. For one, the witness is not just the survivor of Auschwitz. Still, the survivor in any sense post-Auschwitz recognizes the demand made by the *Muselmann,* thus returning speech to the unspeakable, even retroactively, and thus resolving the loss of speech as the horror of the *Muselmann.* Moreover, the witness does not turn away in terror and disgust of the *Muselmann* but is compelled to see what the figure embodies: humanity reduced to mere life, an inhuman entity, unable to see his death coming. The act of witnessing returns humanity to this inhuman figure, returns speech to the living, and – indirectly and even retroactively – returns them to the living.

The significance of the witness returning life to the un-life is one that Agamben saw only as the ultimate accomplishment of the "messianic remnant." What Agamben did not consider were the implications of the cultural erasure caused by the naming of the Jewish inmate as Muslim. What is implied in this naming, and what are the implications? In *The Jew, The Arab,* Gil Anidjar asks why the Jewish inmate has been named a Muslim, noting that it is a term that reflects the Muslim as articulating submission. Still, as indicative of his "pariah" status in the camps, this figure stands as a metaphor for the Jew's status in Europe at the time.[11] While Agamben recognized the irony that the Jew dies a Muslim in the camps, he did not reflect on what his "messianic remnant" would accomplish on these religious signifiers. The fact is, when the inhuman misnamed horror is "tamed" by the human witness who returns what has been lost – his life, his speech, his consciousness – what is conserved is not his Jewishness, but his "life" after death. In effect, Agamben's fantasy of the ethical act of witnessing the *Muselmann* introduces the Christian concept of resurrection.

I suggest that by linking Paul's letter to the Romans about Jesus and repeating Paul's impulse to bring the prophet Isaiah's speeches into his present, Agamben wants to shape his fantasy of salvation through the conservation of life

---

[9] Agamben, 164.

[10] This dynamic of the *Muselmann* and the survivor relies on the bifurcated quality of testimony: the survivor does not testify for herself, alone, but as a voice, or witness, of the collective; in turn, her testimony has voice only if there is a witness, or a collective, listening.

[11] Gil Anidjar, *The Arab, The Jew: A History of the Enemy,* (Stanfield, CA: Stanford California Press, 2003), 144-146.

exemplified by Christian ideology. His perspective is founded on the Christian belief that the Christian God and the Jewish God are one and that Christianity came to fulfill the promise of the Jewish faith. It is important to recognize that for Agamben, the Christian narrative inherits the Old Testament God and thus sublimates the Jewish religious texts into its cultural fabric. In other words, the Christian narrative of eternal life unconsciously affirms Christian supersessionism: God has forgiven the original sin and returned immortality to humankind because Jesus sacrificed his life. Suppose Agamben's messianic remnant is the fantasy denoting the trauma of the camps, and Agamben relies on the principle of eternal life as the conserving power for his fantasy. In that case, we must see that the witness's act of returning life to the *Muselmann* is motivated by Christian ideology. It is unlikely that Agamben is aware of the extent of this Christian bias in his thinking: most readers would not detect it either. For some, though, Agamben's "messianic remnant" fantasy reflects a disturbing second erasure of the Jewish inmate: having already been erased by being named *Muselmann*, the inmate is further erased in his part of the Christian savior paradigm of the resurrection. Notable also is the erasure of Islam's claim to being the newest message of the monotheistic faiths. This outline of the unconscious biases driving Agamben's treatment of the messianic fantasy is meant to highlight how the sectarian principle of the messianic figure is essentially Christian. In Zeitlin's *Beasts*, the Christian bias of the messianic narrative takes on a distinctly racialized bias.

Beasts of the Southern Wild: Take One

Benh Zeitlin's *Beasts of the Southern Wild (2012)* unfolds from the point of view of Hushpuppy, a young girl, who lives with her father in a community of people who live in shacks on the Bayou, known as the Baths, or Bathtub.[12] If the *Muselmann* is the source of Agamben's fantasy of the Nazi death camps, indicative of a kind of Christian effort to "organize" or work through the trauma of the death camps, so Hushpuppy may be seen as the character of the fantasy of this film that is "working through" a trauma. The question, of course, is: what trauma is the fantasy of this film born from?

Set in a not-so-distant future, Hushpuppy and her people are tormented by conditions caused by global warming. The violence of this torment is represented by intermittent depictions of fantastic scenes of beasts (Aurochs) fleeing from melting ice flows. In this wild rural environment, Hushpuppy is left mainly to herself: we see her first playing with little chicks, listening to their heartbeat, and then feeding the animals from the same chicken that she feeds herself. Following the opening scenes of some public festivities in what appears to be

---

[12] This film was based on a short story by Doris Betts and erases much of the particulars of the original, though reconstitutes some of the original elements in interesting ways.

this bucolic, idyllic wilderness, we witness the effects of great winds, ominous clouds, and storm activities, suggesting a storm is threatening to destroy these makeshift homes along the bayou. The audience is, through the course of the film, encouraged to recognize associations between this bayou and the regions of Louisiana devastated by Hurricane Katrina. It is in this global warming context that we read scenes of the Aurochs stampeding with apparent menace as if descending on Hushpuppy's Bathtub. This crisis increases until, at the end of the film, they arrive, and Hushpuppy has this magic effect of making them stop. In that "ethical encounter" with the other, she tells them she needs to look after her own; satisfied, they turn away. In short, the crisis of global warming is averted, with the fabulous quality of a fairytale, where the heroine tames the wild, or, as is suggested by the narrative, the exception that is Hushpuppy, saves humankind.

The film received many accolades. It won the Camera d'Or at Cannes, the Sundance Film Festival Grand Jury Prize – among other awards – and it was nominated for four Academy Awards: Best Motion Picture, Best Performance by an Actress in a Leading Role, Best Achievement Directing, and Best Writing (Adapted Screenplay). These generally positive responses to the film were expressed in scholarship, as well. Negrea associated the film's popularity with contemporary American issues of race and gender: specifically, she argues, the political climate reflected in the filmic world indicates an Obama-worldview of equality. The community of the Bathtub is of mixed race (Black and white), and the story centers on the child Hushpuppy. She may live wild and uncivilized, playing with dirt or starting fires. Still, she is essentially sensitive to the world: she holds a baby chick to her ear, listening to its heartbeat as if it were a telephone, speaking wisdom to her: "Somehow she intuits that every living thing is connected to the next."[13] Hushpuppy's "knowing" beyond her years sets her apart from everyone in her "camp," complicated further by her ambiguous gender: she's walking around with shorts, boots, and a tank top loosely draped over her small shoulders. The sexual ambiguity, Negrea argues, echoes the multi-ethnic community and serves to fulfill the film's promise as per Brecht's political idea that "Movies do not just mirror the culture of any given time; they also create it."[14] This film is not about an existing community but some future world in which the most unlikely subject will save the world from humankind, and that unlikely subject – in this case – is a little Black girl.

---

[13] Irinia Negrea, "Mom, I think I broke Something: Thinking about the Environment in Benh Zeitlin's *Beasts of the Southern Wild,*" in *Movies in the Age of Obama: The Era of Post-Racial and Neo-Racist Cinema,* ed. David Garrett Izzo (New York: Rowman and Littefield, 2014), 133.
[14] Ibid., 132.

So, Hushpuppy is an exceptional little girl in a place called the Baths that echoes a kind of camp of the disenfranchised.

Negrea correctly emphasizes that the association between the film's "apocalyptic storm" and Hurricane Katrina is necessary in order to recognize the film's force for correction. In contrast, Louisiana citizens suffered very real racial and class discrimination by America's governing parties and agencies affected by Hurricane Katrina. This alternative community on screen –independent of the mainland – shared racial differences in supporting each other before, during, and after the disaster. In this sense, Negrea suggests, the film gestures to Obama's focus on non-discrimination in government and beyond, promoting activism on climate change at the grass-roots level.[15] The crisis that is real is global warming: in the film, this impending disaster is represented by the Aurochs, who rush to meet Hushpuppy. As the Queen of the Tub, she saves her family and herself from the invasion of the beasts, thus proving that even a child can save humankind from climate change. For Negrea, this film is a positive force: it reflects the dynamic of inclusion through the racially diverse members of this "camp." It promises a future of salvation from global warming through the generosity and wisdom of a young Black girl known as the Queen of the Tub.

In contrast to the positive responses to the film, as exemplified by Negrea's review, bell hooks are highly critical. She claims that the fantastic aesthetic of the film obscures how fundamentally racist and especially sexist it is: "It is precisely this mythic focus that deflects attention away from egregious sub-textual narratives present in the film… no racial talk, no racial discourses, disturbs the peace."[16] This is to say that the move to resolve racial and social issues by showing a bi-racial, socially mixed community is simplistic and dangerously racist. More problematic is that Hushpuppy's father, Wink, is a stereotype of the American Black man: abusive and lazy, an alcoholic and lustful womanizer. As king, he shows this Bathtub to be as misogynistic as the mainland, unironically teaching Hushpuppy how to be an abusive bully. According to Hooks, he shows her no love whatsoever.

Hushpuppy's gender ambiguity, hooks contends, is extremely problematic. Far from neutralizing her sexual identity, her appearance as cute and tom-boyish in underwear and a tank top that barely clothes her dangerously eroticizes her pre-pubescent body as "transgender."[17] Her trip to Elysium with the sailors continues the misogynistic narrative: hooks sees no value in bringing the girls into this world where men are using women for casual sex.

---

[15] Ibid., 139.
[16] bell hooks, "No Love in the Wild." *NewBlackMan (in Exile)*, September 5, 2012. https://www.newblackmaninexile.net/2012/09/bell-hooks-no-love-in-wild.html.
[17] Ibid.

Notable here is hooks' middle-class reaction against organized prostitution, and one might argue that the film actually goes against this class type by representing the women as caring mother-type figures. If they are mothers, though, where are their children? This absence suggests that Elysium is a floating jail and a counter-point to the Bathtub and may, in fact, be a thin layer of positive gendering over a very racist and sexist story, thus confirming what hooks' defines as the fundamentally conservative quality of the narration.

Hooks identifies the greatest weakness of the film as centering on Hushpuppy's apparent mental health despite her wild world and parent-less upbringing:

> There is no love, no hands holding on, just a blank emptiness onto which any mark can be placed, any fantastical story written. All along the way, Hushpuppy has not been at the center of *Beasts*… She is marginalized; she is a backup singer. No wonder, then, so few listeners fail to choose a standpoint where they might witness her suffering or hear her ongoing anguished lament.[18]

The overwhelming emotion of hooks' conclusion here is audible: she feels strongly that only those who have not experienced racism or sexism would find this film heartwarming. This is to say that only someone who has never suffered abuse as a child – abandonment, discrimination, or hunger – can believe that a child growing up under those conditions could suddenly be the recipient of love or even the giver of love. The only way one might conceive of this possibility is as the divine possibility in the shape of Aurochs. Notable is the fact that, as a "backup" singer, she can be heard and lamented, but that is all she is. Also notable is that the film reverts to a weak reference to some divine force.

Hooks' critique of the film offers some insight into thinking through Agamben's principle of the messianic remnant in contemporary political terms. Only someone who is not a *Muselmann* could actually believe in the power to see in his marginal existence, a human-centered power of the witness to bring salvation to all humanity. Moreover, suppose the fantasy of the "messianic remnant" is a conservative principle. In that case, we can see even more clearly what hooks argues is the "conservative agenda" of this film's narrative that insists "that only the strong survive, that disease weeds out the weak (i.e., the slaughter of Native Americans), that nature chooses excluding and including."[19] For Agamben, the strength of the conservative is enabled by the survivor's ethical act of witnessing the *Muselmann*: this ethics returns life. In terms of hooks' interpretation of conservative, Hushpuppy's positivity makes it possible for her to survive both her raging mom and her alcoholic father without harm and

---

[18] Ibid.
[19] Ibid.

engage in that ethical encounter with the Aurochs that saves humanity from destruction. Reading hooks with Agamben, we can see that the conservative quality of each fantasy relies on the one who has faith in the power of witnessing, an audience member who believes in the power of humanity to rise above hardship, who can see Hushpuppy as a savior. As the *homo sacer* of the Bath, she allows us, the audience, to "rope her" into the narrative of salvation for humanity only because we believe in this rope; there are many, such as hooks, who do not.

Hushpuppy is, in Agamben's terms, of the *homo sacer* in that she is the marginalized figure: marginal from the mainland; marginal as racially Black; marginal as a very young girl; marginal as isolated in the wild; marginal as gifted with the ability to speak to Aurochs. Through her, we – the survivor/audience – may witness and bring about a messianic potential, excepting that she is also merely a character, representing actual people who have been marginalized in American history. She drives the fantasy of some trauma that we cannot access directly, much in the same way the *Muselmann* is the *Homo sacer* that points to the remainder of the "encounter with the real." She is also the effect of a textual translation, specifically Doris Bett's short story, "Beasts of the Southern Wild." The extent to which this film "conserves" the qualities of the original short story of feminist and civil rights politics is worth exploring.

Beasts of the Southern Wild: Take Two

Despite the fact that the 2012 film and the original short story share the same title, seeing a connection between them is a bit of a stretch. There is no girl in the short story; moreover, while the Bayou is set in a marginalized and impoverished area, the short story has two locations: the white middle-class American neighborhood and a fantastic representation of southern slavery. The similarity between the film and the story is emphasized by hooks' observation of Betts' narrative: it "has one of the most sexist and racist representations of black masculinity in contemporary southern literature."[20] The fact is, the Black man in Betts's short story is as much a stereotype as Hushpuppy's father is. Ironically, where Hushpuppy's father is a stereotype of the misogynist alcoholic black man, Sam is the ultimate expression of the black man living a white man's life. It is the detail of this difference that explains how the conservative quality of the film observed by hooks is more obvious in the story and can potentially lead to answering the question: who is served by the film's fantasy?

The short story, published in 1973, weaves a first-person fantasy sequence with third-person realism regarding the same protagonist named Carol. She is introduced first through her fantasy of being a white slave woman chosen by a Black enslaver – someone like Sidney Poitier – to be a companion in his little

---

[20] Ibid.

mansion.[21] In the realist narrative, Carol lives a middle-class life: mother of two sons with a conservative, Republican, non-intellectual husband who owns an upholstery shop. The lack of intellectual stimulation at home is exacerbated by the quality of thought by her high school students on the poetry of Wordsworth or Coleridge. Perhaps her frustration at work is simply exemplifying her frustration in the marriage: her husband claims that she was lucky to be married to him, and she references that he has implied she is not only reserved but also frigid, i.e., "Ice-box."[22] The connection between her real life and the fantasy is made explicit when the husband mentions the "Nigger couch," saying, "It smelled so bad, Pete moved it in the back lot and tore it down out there. Beats me why they smell different. It's in the sweat, I guess."[23] This scene triggers an episode in the fantasy when Sam, the black enslaver, kisses Carol as he leaves to go to bed. She notes, "… there is a smell: yes, it is sweetish."[24] Not only do we see in Carol's fantasy of Sam a counterpoint to her husband's off-handed racism, but Sam's politeness and reserve sexually arouse her, contradicting the misogynist complaint of her "ice-box" frigidity. Sam is not only polite and caring, but his sense of chivalry leads him to offer to kill the man who raped Carol. In the fantasy, Carol names her husband in the realist narrative, and in that fantasy, the rapist is killed. The dialogue between the fantasy and reality within this story shows that racial and gender issues relevant to Carol are addressed, but solely for Carol's benefit.

Considering the feminine-centered perspective of this story, hooks' claim that this story is both sexist and racist regarding American Black masculinity is probably obvious to all contemporary readers. And I think claiming that hooks' condemnation is somewhat anachronistic would be fair. Yet, looking at how this story offers its contemporary audience any inkling of a feminist position allows us to look more closely at what kind of feminist politics is driving this story. That is, the dynamic between Carol's fantasy and reality shows a rage with restrictions of gender as imposed by the dominant hegemonic patriarchy. There is a feminist agenda in this story, but it is strikingly white. As a woman repressed by middle-class expectations of mothering and teaching children, sexing, and serving the husband, there is no escape except to carry out patricide in the fantasy. Doing so through the racial other becomes another part of the agenda: the figure of an inferior racial class killing the father/husband can be seen as a more politically radical act of resistance – if we could believe that Sam is actually a Black man and not just a fantasy of a white woman.

---

[21] Doris Betts, "Beasts of the Southern Wild," *Carolina Quarterly*, Spring 1973, 46.
[22] Ibid., 53.
[23] Ibid.
[24] Ibid., 55.

The white woman's fantasy uses anti-racist politics to stake the terms of her feminist liberation. This fantasy world of white slavery, wherein white women are enslaved, maltreated, abused, and raped by black enslavers, finds resolution in the story of a white enslaved person saved by a black man. He is a university dean, educated and gentle. His sensitivity to human frailty, as expressed in how he treats his white woman – giving her food, books to read, leisure to do with as she pleases, letting her initiate sex – means that he can feel for an enslaved person, but only intellectually. He is rich and cultured, as any white man could be. Yet, he has a body that arouses her. She uses a lot of language to describe his muscles, obviously paying attention: "I follow on the stairs, watching his thighs when he lifts each leg, how the muscles catch."[25] Notable is how visible his skin is, how it ripples, and how it attracts attention. Her interest in his muscles is erotic. This black enslaver is the right combination of animal and intellect and a counterfoil of Carol's husband in reality. Nowhere do we see the reality of Black slavery in this Sam: he is a cypher for Carol's desires.

As a cypher, Sam is so shallow or empty that the feminist/anti-racist narrative highlights the political and ethical failures of his character. For one, when Sam, the black intellectual, saves a white woman, he saves her because she is educated, implying that those who are not educated have no chance of being "chosen" by him. Strikingly, Sam has no Black woman as a partner. Most importantly, he saves only one woman of all the enslaved people and leaves the rest to suffer. This would suggest that Carol's fantasy of the Black man may as well be a white enslaver for his lack of moral outrage at the plight of all the enslaved people in the society she lives in. If we put more pressure on this "character," we can see that behind his middle-class life, he continues with a sense of privilege (the enslaved person deserves to be an enslaved person) but is also aware of his sexual prowess as a Black man for a white woman: "And you never had pleasure? From a black?"[26] Notice that the term "black" is dissociated from the word "man," and all of these terms are expressed in this repressed dissociation from "pleasure." This repression might be in the voice of Sam, but this story is not Sam's story; it is Carol's story, a frigid white woman who is aroused less by being "chosen" than by being enslaved to a Black man. His Blackness is expedient, as is the slave allusion, which ultimately points to racism underlying the white feminist agenda, targeting the white patriarchy. That the Black man turns on a white man's wife is probably the ultimate blow to the ego. What is playing in Carol's fantasy are two desires: that the Black man can ruin the white man's sense of on a white woman's appropriation privilege and that a Black man will

---

[25] Ibid., 51.
[26] Ibid., 54.

change her "ice-box" problem. This narrative is centered of a slave narrative for erotic satisfaction and, in that sense, is perverted.

Betts' fantasy plays with slavery as a simple game of inversion, supposing that slavery narratives can strike at two political crises at the same time: the oppression of women and the oppression of Black people. As a woman's fantasy, it simplifies racial oppression as a class issue so that a woman's erotic fantasy occludes the reality of slavery. Meanwhile, the Black man steps into the shoes of the white man as if he has never suffered in his life and conveniently becomes the white woman's salvation at the expense of all others who have suffered, and without any reflection on the Black woman. These narrative changes nothing in our reality: the story maintains the very power conditions that force this middle-class white woman to be enslaved to the men around her, and it also reinforces her superiority to the black men in her community because Sam has no interest in changing the conditions that oppress women. In creating the petri-dish of this narrative, Betts is not interested in fighting on behalf of civil rights nor the privilege that she thrives in. As a white woman, she is motivated by seeing the white man squirm with disgust and envy because of her fantasy of the Black man's "smell"; she is interested in exploring the white woman's racialized erotic desire, wherein her chosen-ness is not politically motivated to address racial issues, but is simply an unconscious expression of sexual repression. In these ways, Betts' story is extremely conservative in the sense that there is resistance to change.

The Messianic Fantasy

By transposing this second-wave American feminist narrative into the trans-racial narrative promised by *Beasts of the Southern Wild*, we can see that the former's conservative quality has not been dismantled by the representation of Blackness in the latter but, in fact, is sustained. Carol – the slave woman protagonist who only wants her needs met and will use racialized narratives that save her and satisfy her – is recreated in the narrative of Hushpuppy, the young "transgender" or androgynous Black girl, who by encountering the "beast" of climate change, tames it, and thus assures the future of humanity. As a savior, Hushpuppy is more like Sam. And Sam saving the white woman is the white woman's fantasy. Yet, who is to say that Hushpuppy is not simply an expression of an American white person's fantasy? Yet, what is that fantasy?

We can begin to explore what the film's fantasy conserves by comparing the characters in the short story and the film. If Betts' story is about patriarchal hegemony and women's liberation, and the film is about the devastating effects of global warming, then neither addresses the elephant in the room: the racial subject as evident in Sam and Hushpuppy. Sam functions in Carol's narrative as an inversion of American slavery, thus sustaining white hegemony; Hushpuppy's father, as hooks observed, perpetuates the stereotype of the misogynist, violent, and alcoholic Black man, though Hushpuppy complicates the racial stereotype. Hushpuppy may be Black, but she does not live her racialized Blackness: her racial identity, in fact, is as superficial as Sam's racial identity. Hushpuppy is an ambivalently gendered subject, which – one supposes – shows her in a complicated relation to Betts' concept of feminism. In effect, you might say Hushpuppy is the conflation of Sam and Carol with their complicated gendered racial subjectivities. With respect to the salvation narrative, we can see that while the deracialized Sam is a savior of the white woman, Hushpuppy is a de-racialized and somewhat feminized savior of "everyone." Where Sam's race is used to expose and torture the white man, Hushpuppy is used to appease the white Americans by saving them from environmental disasters. The fact is that Hushpuppy's salvation centers on the climate crisis, which means that the issue of race has disappeared in ways that reinforce the racial obfuscation apparent in Carol's feminist fantasy. Does the fantasy of the short story belong to the repressed white woman, whose fantasy is manifested by Hushpuppy's role in the film?

Let's take seriously the association the film makes between Hushpuppy in the Baths and residents of Louisiana during Hurricane Katrina. We see the specter of the class issue as fundamental to the story. Hushpuppy's life points to poverty, including the very real poverty of the residents in Louisiana who the government abandoned, left to drown, or starve, all of which flies in the face of the democratic promise of equality for all. Underlying the economic class inequality is another more insidious issue: racism. Deep within America's treatment of poverty is the stigmatism of racial discrimination running through the centuries since Southern plantation culture exploited Black workforce as animal labor. I stress that the labor is associated with the animal to highlight a pattern of racism and slavery that Hannah Arendt observes about the Boer treatment of enslaved people in South Africa. In *The Origins of Totalitarianism*, Arendt writes: "When the Boers, in their fright and misery, decided to use these savages as though they were just another form of animal life, they embarked upon a process which could only end with their degeneration into a white race living beside and together with black races."[27] The racism the Boers promoted was essentially anti-Christian since it negated the "common origin of men."[28] While white racism in America is ideologically elitist, America is still a Christian nation with ideals of democratic equality among all citizens. Thus, if the American dream relies on the Christian promise of opportunity for all, then Hushpuppy articulates not Black America's emancipation but white America's Christian guilt.

---

[27] Hannah Arendt, *The Origins of Totalitarianism* (Cleveland, OH: Meridian Books, 1962), 194.
[28] Ibid., 195.

What is accomplished for the audience when watching Hushpuppy save her people from the effects of global warming? Drawing from bell hooks' criticism of the film, we can say that Hushpuppy, as the protagonist, flatters the victim into thinking they can represent a Christian story of the weak inheriting the earth. Meanwhile, her role as a messianic figure highlights her exceptionality in race and class, which reinforces how the Christian values of equality (i.e., anyone can be a president) is a story that forgives the perpetrator. The white American audience is forgiven their lifestyle, which is at the expense of the underclass; they are absolved of culpability in abandoning the poor classes, which is rooted in the anti-Christian values seeded in slave history. In short, Hushpuppy may be seen as the figure of a salvation fantasy caused by the *objet a*, or the remainder, of the real of America's racialized history, wherein the trauma represented in the film is not that of the racialized enslaved person, but that of white America's role as an enslaver. It is this status as the perpetrator of racial crimes that explains white America's compulsive resistance to resolving racialized poverty – a kind of denial of the facts – apparent in the film's conserving interest in reinforcing its putative Christian ideals of equality, especially considering the social and environmental disasters of Hurricane Katrina, followed by the economic downturn of 2008.

If Agamben's *Muselmann* is the figure for whom death was not visible – for whom there was no language – compelling the witness to accept culpability for the crimes against humanity in the death camps and thus build the fantasy of the "messianic remnant," the trauma of the camps generated a fantasy that conserved the blessing of the Christian resurrection. The *Muselmann* is brought back to life in the eyes of the witness. The *homo sacer* of Hushpuppy, the young Black girl who – orphaned, hungry, isolated, innocent, and illiterate – appears to show us a Christian narrative of forgiveness of what white America has done because of its racist origins. But Hushpuppy is a character who does not see what we, the audience, see: that her world is the garbage pit of obscene wealth. In watching her, a very young Black girl, accept her lot in life so willingly, so happily, we, the white American audience members, can believe that she is not accusing us of creating her little Bath; in her, we can bury our guilt in the messianic fabric of the hope she represents. Hope was enabled by those who survived Hurricane Katrina and the slave trade, forgetting those who did not survive. In effect, since Hushpuppy is not hurt by her skin color, the centuries of racial discrimination have been erased, literally. She is the protagonist of the fantasy generated by the *objet a* of slavery, and as such, expresses white America's trauma of slave history. As a character, she ensures the film conserves the quality of life made by capitalism's hunger to exploit natural resources and human beings for individual privileged comforts.

Conclusion

In Lacan's terms, the fantasy does not tell us what happened since what happened is that shock that was missed; the fantasy, in reflecting an "organizing" impulse of the trauma, signals that trauma happened. The person's fantasy is organized around something leftover from the trauma. As much as Agamben's process of the "witnessing" of the *Muselmann* speaks where no speech is left or returns humanity where it has been erased, the fantasy that plays out is the conservation of life, in Christian terms, through the resurrection. The value of the fantasy for the analyst is that, first, it identifies that a trauma happened, and second, it tells the analyst what is important for the analysis. The point of analysis is to see that there is a fantasy and to recognize that the fantasy is a "conservative" crutch that can be discarded. In short, the objective of the analytic dialogue between the analyst and the analysand is for the analysand to move beyond the fantasy, otherwise known as "traverse the fantasy." Thus, Agamben's organizing of Levi's horror was motivated by the conservative impulse to resurrect the *Muselmann* from his obscene death, which is not real. Yet, of the real, and defined as the "messianic remnant." We can suggest that the *Muselmann* fantasy aims to traverse the fantasy of messianism as a resurrection.

She can hear beyond human hearing, which sets Hushpuppy apart from the rest. Hushpuppy listens to the world in this make-believe way, which emphasizes what is poignant about her ongoing dialogue with her dead mother. In Hushpuppy's ability to witness the exceptions around her – namely her dead mother, her suffering father, and especially the Aurochs – we find various disjunctions: the disjunction between humankind and beast, between the living and the dead, and between the present and the future disaster. In that disjunction, we may see a messianic remnant; indeed, Hushpuppy's witnessing of the Aurochs indicates a messianic fulfillment. Yet, in whose interest is this messianic fabric being woven?

Bibliography

Agamben, Giorgio. *Remnants of Auschwitz: The Witness and the Archive.* Translated by Daniel Heller-Roazen. New York: Zone Books, 2002.

Arendt, Hannah. *The Origins of Totalitarianism.* Cleveland, OH: Meridian Books, 1962.

Anidjar, Gil. *The Arab, The Jew: A History of the Enemy.* Stanfield, CA: Stanford California Press, 2003.

Betts, Doris. "Beasts of the Southern Wild." *Carolina Quarterly*, Spring 1973.

hooks, bell. "No Love in the Wild." *NewBlackMan (in Exile)*, September 5, 2012. https://www.newblackmaninexile.net/2012/09/bell-hooks-no-love-in-wild.html.

Lacan, Jacques. *Four Fundamental Concepts of Psychoanalysis: Seminar XI.* Edited by Jacques Alain Miller, translated by Alan Sheridan. New York: W. W. Norton and Company, 1998.

Levi Primo. *Survival in Auschwitz: The Nazi Assault on Humanity.* Translated by Stuart Woolf. New York: Simon and Schuster, 1996.

Negrea, Irinia. "Mom, I think I broke Something: Thinking about the Environment in Benh Zeitlin's *Beasts of the Southern Wild.*" In *Movies in the Age of Obama: The Era of Post-Racial and Neo-Racist Cinema*, edited by David Garret Izzo, 131-148. New York: Rowman and Littlefield, 2014.

Zeitlin, Benh, dir. *Beasts of the Southern Wild.* 2012; Toronto: Entertainment One Films Canada.

Contributors

Layla AlAmmar

Layla AlAmmar is a writer from Kuwait with a PhD in Arab women's fiction and literary trauma theory. She received a Master's degree in Creative Writing from the University of Edinburgh and has published two novels. She has written journal articles on the fiction of Adania Shibli as well as the collection Palestine +100, and she is currently co-editing a special issue, *Wombs and Tombs: Hauntings and Generational Trauma in Arab Women's Writing*.

Rachel Dale

Rachel Dale holds a Master's degree in English from Brandeis University (2020) and is currently pursuing a Ph.D. in contemporary global Anglophone literature at the same institution. Concurrently, she teaches trauma treatment and PTSD at the Van Loan School of Professional Studies at Endicott College. Her dissertation examines the detrimental effects of internationally funded industrial and economic development projects, drawing on the perspectives of contemporary realist authors like Arundhati Roy, Amitav Ghosh, and NoViolet Bulawayo, among others. She has been awarded several fellowships and grants, including the Shirle Dorothy Robbins Creative Writing Prize in 2021.

Maryam Ghodrati

Maryam Ghodrati holds a Ph.D. in Comparative Literature from the University of Massachusetts Amherst and currently serves as Affiliated Faculty at Emerson College in Boston. Her research encompasses trauma studies, literary theory, women's studies, film studies, and contemporary Middle Eastern and diaspora studies. She teaches courses on trauma in creative imagination, body politics, literature and social justice, and gender and sexuality in global literature. Her translations of war poetry have been featured in a special issue titled "Casualty" in *The Massachusetts Review*. Her article, titled "Narrative Materialization of Traumatic Memory" is under review for publication in a 2024 special issue of Iranian Studies by Cambridge University Press.

Nora E. H. Parr

Nora Parr is a research fellow at the University of Birmingham and the Center for Lebanese Studies. She is a co-investigator on the Rights for Time research network and a co-editor of *Middle Eastern Literature*. She is the author of the *Novel Palestine: Nation through the Works of Ibrahim Nasrallah* (University of California Press, 2023).

Concetta Principe

Concetta Principe's current scholarship focuses on the relationship between culture and madness from a Lacanian perspective. Her article, "Authorial Rights and the Cultural Economy of Madness," was published in 2022 in *Psychoanalytische Perspectieven*. She is co-editor of *From Cogito to Covid: A Rethinking of Lacan's "Science and Truth"* (Palgrave MacMillan, 2022) and author of a chapter in *From Cogito to Covid*, "The Truth of Lacan's Name of the Father: A Reconsiderati on of the 'truth' in 'Science and Truth.'" Her research has appeared in *Psychoanalysis, Culture and Society, Psychoanalytic Discourse/ Discours Psychoanalytique, Journal of Cultural Research* and *The Bible and Critical Theory*. Alongside her scholarly publications, she is a peer reviewer for *Religion and Literature, English Studies in Canada*, and *Topia*. She is a member of the Equity Committee at Trent University in Durham, Canada, where she is an Assistant Professor teaching literature and writing studies.

James E. Young

James E. Young is Distinguished University Professor of English and Judaic Studies Emeritus at the University of Massachusetts Amherst and the Founding Director of the Institute for Holocaust, Genocide, and Memory Studies at UMass Amherst. Young has also taught at New York University as a Dorot Professor of English and Hebrew/Judaic Studies (1984-88), at Bryn Mawr College in the History of Religion, and the University of Washington, Harvard University, and Princeton University as a visiting professor. He received his Ph.D. from the University of California Santa Cruz in 1983. He is the author of *Writing and Rewriting the Holocaust* (Indiana University Press, 1988), *The Texture of Memory* (Yale University Press, 1993), which won the National Jewish Book Award in 1994, *At Memory's Edge: After-images of the Holocaust in Contemporary Art and Architecture* (Yale University Press, 2000), and *The Stages of Memory: Reflections on Memorial Art, Loss, and the Spaces Between* (University of Massachusetts Press, 2016), which won the National Council for Public History Book Award for 2017. He was also the Guest Curator of an exhibition at the Jewish Museum in New York City, entitled "The Art of Memory: Holocaust Memorials in History" (March - August 1994, with venues in Berlin and Munich, September 1994 - June 1995) and was the editor of *The Art of Memory* (Prestel Verlag, 1994), the exhibition catalog for this show. In 1997, Professor Young was appointed by the Berlin Senate to the five-member *Findungskommission* for Germany's national "Memorial to Europe's Murdered Jews," which selected Peter Eisenman's design, finished and dedicated in May 2005. More recently, he was appointed to the jury for the "National 9/11 Memorial" design competition, won by Michael Arad and Peter Walker in 2004 and opened on September 11th, 2011. Professor Young has written widely on public art, memorials, and national memory. His articles, reviews, and Op-Ed essays have appeared in *The New York Times* Magazine, Book Review, and Op-Ed pages, *The Los Angeles Times*, *The Chicago Tribune*, *The Forward*, and *Frankfurter Allgemeine Zeitung*, among other newspapers, as well as in scholarly journals such as *Critical Inquiry*, *Representations*, *New Literary History*, *PMLA*, *Partisan Review*, *The Yale Journal of Criticism*, *Annales*, *SAQ*, *History and Theory*, *Harvard Design Magazine*, *Jewish Social Studies*, *Contemporary Literature*, *History and Memory*, *The Chronicle of Higher Education*, *Holocaust and Genocide Studies*, *Prooftexts*, *The Jewish Quarterly*, *Tikkun*, and *Slate*, among dozens of other journals and collected volumes. His books and articles have been published in German, French, Hebrew, Japanese, and Swedish editions. Professor Young is the recipient of numerous awards and fellowships, including a Guggenheim Fellowship, ACLS Fellowship, NEH Exhibition planning, implementation, and research grants, Memorial Foundation for Jewish Culture Grants, an American Philosophical Society Grant, and a Yad Hanadiv Fellowship at the Hebrew University in Jerusalem, among others.

Acknowledgments

As the editors of *Embodied Testimonies, Gendered Memories, and the Poetics of Trauma*, we would like to extend our profound gratitude to the following individuals and groups whose support and contributions were invaluable in making this book a reality:

The amazing authors, Dr. James Young, Dr. Layla AlAmmar, Dr. Nora Parr, and Dr. Concetta Principe, for sharing their research with us and for their patience and trust throughout the process.

The editorial staff at Vernon Press – especially Irene Benavides, Blanca Caro Duran, and Argiris Legatos – for their assistance and direction as we have been working on this collection.

Dr. Moira Inghilleri, Professor of Translation and Interpreting Studies and Comparative Literature and Director of the UMass Cornerstone Initiative at the University of Massachusetts Amherst, for her invaluable guidance and feedback.

Samantha Whittle, Dr. Ghodatri's diligent research assistant and a graduate student of Comparative Literature at the University of Massachusetts Amherst, for her meticulous attention to detail and dedication to this project.

Dr. Amir Barati of Texas Tech University, thank you for your insightful contribution to the conference proposal that inspired this collection.

John Halaka, visual artist, documentary filmmaker, and Professor of Visual Arts at the University of San Diego in California, graciously shared his valuable time to engage in several insightful and illuminating conversations about art's role in resistance to political oppression within colonized and diaspora communities.

Minoo Emami, a multidisciplinary artist whose artistic endeavors have bridged the gap between art and advocacy, graciously shared her art for the cover of this collection.

Dr. Emilie Diouf, Assistant Professor of English at Brandeis University, for her compassionate guidance and feedback.

Dr. Jennifer Ellis West, Associate Professor of English and Director of the Core Rhetoric Seminar at Samford University, for her insights on trauma studies and for modeling the ethic of care and attention that informs this scholarship.

Dr. Dominick Knowles, lecturer at the University of Massachusetts Boston, Poetry Editor at Protean Magazine, and Academic Director at the Clemente

Course in the Humanities (Boston), for sharing their expertise regarding the editorial and publication process.

We would also like to extend our gratitude to our incredible families and dedicated partners. Their encouragement and understanding have made this accomplishment possible.

Finally, Ms. H.D., an extraordinary survivor of a devastating chemical attack, offers a poignant and courageous testament to the harsh realities of enduring and surviving the aftermath of such a traumatic event. Through her conversations and introspective diaries, she provides a unique and invaluable perspective on the physical and psychological challenges faced by survivors of war, shedding light on the profound impact of such experiences on an individual's life and the broader human understanding of resilience in the face of extreme adversity.

Index